MONTGOMERY'S BUSES

An Empire of Independents

by

Brian Poole

THE OAKWOOD PRESS

British Library Cataloguing in Publication Data
A Record for this book is available from the British Library
ISBN 978 0 85361 694 8

Typeset by Oakwood Graphics.
Repro by PKmediaworks, Cranborne, Dorset.
Printed by Cambrian Printers, Aberystwyth, Ceredigion.

This photograph dates from the 1950s and shows three buses that were parked overnight on the site at Tregynon. Walter Davies took his PSV test in Guy EP 9502. This is the only local photograph located as yet where a Sentinel (CEP 247) is carrying the dark blue livery of Mid-Wales Motorways. *Eddie Francis and Mid-Wales Motorways*

Front cover: The classic Bedford OB bus parked on a gradient to collect two ladies on their way to Newtown market. The Newtown to Mochdre only ran on Tuesdays leaving Mochdre at 9.35 am and returning from Newtown at 2.56 pm. There were two other services on Tuesday and two on Saturday and these continued through Mochdre higher in the hills at Pentre. This is a typical route for the light bus moving along narrow lanes and crossing several valleys with steep gradients on blind curves. The first owner was the Bristol Omnibus Company. The driver on this route was Cyril Haines.
Eddie Francis and Mid-Wales Motorways

By the same author (with Lewis Cozens and R.W. Kidner)
The Mawddwy, Van & Kerry Branches (Oakwood Press, 2004)

Published by The Oakwood Press (Usk), P.O. Box 13, Usk, Mon., NP15 1YS.
E-mail: sales@oakwoodpress.co.uk
Website: www.oakwoodpress.co.uk

Contents

A tramcar was constructed for the 1912 Newtown carnival. The supposed journey was Newtown to Tregynon and the conductor with no electricity to conduct would shout 'Last car to Tregynon, penny all the way'. Few Montgomeryshire people would have experienced a tramway ride. The nearest small system was the Wrexham to Rhosllannerchrugog tramway. The nearest extensive systems were either Birmingham or Liverpool.

David Pugh/Newtown Local History Group Collection

Mid-Wales Motorways Dodge EP 6595 is at the Gravel Park loading passengers for New Mills. The corner left may show one of the Tilling Stephens on the wartime book. This could be a bleak place to wait for buses during heavy rain and wind. The driver is thought to be Bernie Williams.

The Omnibus Society

Introduction

Montgomeryshire is now one of the three components of the County of Powys created in 1974 from the three central Welsh counties of Brecknockshire, Radnorshire and Montgomeryshire. One premise for the then Welsh County reorganization was to attempt to get an Authority with population over 100,000; therefore this huge geographical area with its population of just below 100,000 was created. Many people still think of the old counties. It is the very low density of population throughout this upland area that has always caused and continues to pose, different transport problems. It was and remains a county of small businesses heavily dependent on service, agriculture, forestry and quarry extraction. Tourism has become important and may benefit from improved passenger transport to supplement that of the private car. Therefore these Central Welsh Counties have a different bus industry from the mainstream urban and suburban systems. Our title is therefore 'Montgomery Buses, An Empire of Independents'. Two county towns could be joined to give 'A Bedford in Montgomery' and the reason for this from about 1930 to 1995 will unfold later.

Research often starts with a concept for a single essay and this is the case with this tome. There is a local historical society with a magazine entitled *The Newtonian*. Many articles recall aspects of the town and surrounds from the older citizens. I therefore interviewed an older friend known for 40 years. Bill Cross was the young fitter when Mid-Wales Motorways was created in 1937. I immediately realised that there was much more information hidden within the families of the Montgomeryshire bus/coach industry and this has been traced. The information given far exceeds that for this volume. Many have gone to much effort to find old documents and photographs. One cannot express enough thanks for their kindness. It is hoped that this is not only a valued local (unusual) history, but will also have a far wider readership with people who are interested in the bus and coach industry. 'Bysiau bach cefn gwlad Maldwyn' or Montgomeryshire rural buses has a different perspective from the counties dominated by one of the large provincial companies. Many people since the 1960s will have often seen a bus from their car but rarely travelled in a local bus. In Montgomeryshire, it would have been rare to have seen a stage bus, let alone travel on it.

Brian Poole
Newtown

Place Names and Spellings

The earlier bus timetables show many names only in English or with an anglicised spelling such a Voel, Van or Vaynor instead of Y Foel, Y Fan or Faenor. Powys County Council timetable information is bilingual and an example follows:

Ceri, Eglwys	1017	Kerry, Church
Y Drenewydd, Gorsaf Bws	1027	Newtown, Bus Station

Most place names are Welsh but are used in both languages. No attempt is made to translate Llanidloes or Carno or Trewern. There are fewer examples where the English is used for both languages such as Four Crosses where the name may have derived from the Shropshire Turnpike Trust. It is only a few miles from Four Crosses into Shropshire where the Welsh names are retained. Examples are Llynclys and Porth-y-waen.

The convention is now to spell in modern Welsh except where the names are very different such as Welshpool/Y Trallwng or Guilsfield/Cegidfa or Cemmaes Road/Glantwymyn. Tradition retains spelling in both languages such as Kerry/Ceri even though the sound is identical. This can cause odd results and debate such as Bettws or Betws where the word is derived from Saxon for bead house (chapel) where prayers would be said with a rosary. There is a Bettisfield east of Oswestry. Both local parties would understand certain bilingual names while a Welsh speaker would rarely use such examples as Buttington/Talybont or Chirbury/Llanfynhonwyn. Road signs are bilingual but never use the Welsh word for a community over the border in Shropshire yet most Welsh speakers will naturally refer to Croesoswallt for Oswestry or Amwythig for Shrewsbury. This may help explain why a train appears at Amwythig station with 'Caerdydd Canolog' on the indicator screen alternating with 'Cardiff Central'.

The same changes will be seen in modern OS Maps where Dyffryn Dyfi now appears alongside Dovey Valley. Certain names contain past transport history in either language. Sarn derives from a paved crossing of waterlogged ground dating back to Roman times. There is no longer any railway at the end of Station Road in Llanfyllin. The problem is continually faced when writing the narrative for this book. Maybe all forms of spelling are correct as all are within recent or current usage. The town bus trundles between Pinefields and Maesyrhandir. Few have concern that it will soon be at Newtown Bus Station beside the Latin 'fluvius' or the Brythonic 'afon' or the Norman 'river' as the Germanic 'flud' has a specific modern meaning with the Roman option of Sabrina or the Welsh choice of Hafren or the English Severn.

Chapter One

Setting the Scene

Montgomeryshire is not unique. There are other areas of rural Britain, including Ireland, with similar stories. No large town or city dominates the county. Road traffic was, and remains, less intense. One is far more likely to meet a sheep on the road than a roundabout or traffic lights. There are no motorways or even dual carriage sections. The topography and weather of an upland area pose further problems. The area is not watertight like the Isle of Wight or Anglesey. The boundary is therefore artificial and fluid so that a company in the east will trade in Shropshire, the area south of Newtown and Llanidloes moves easily into Radnorshire and Machynlleth borders on both the old Cardiganshire and Merioneth. The town of Oswestry in Shropshire was and still is the natural point of communication for the north-east of the county and could almost claim to be a Welsh town.

The overall pattern of bus operation will now unfold comparing the mainstream development of urban/suburban Britain compared with the differences in Montgomeryshire. A stage route indicates that a service is provided at a certain time and on certain days. The passenger is entitled to board if conditions are met and there is space available; few travel the whole distance. This was the basis of the stagecoach although the fare was well beyond the means of the rural labourer. Montgomeryshire had no political, industrial or military centre. Roads were close to being non-existent and the first turnpike set a pattern of travel out of the county from Welshpool to both Oswestry and Shrewsbury. Goods such as lead and copper were low volume/high value and moved on pack ponies and cart to Poolquay for transport in trows down the River Severn or to Derwenlas for coastal shipping along the Welsh coast. Any journey further than a few miles on foot would not have been undertaken. The only common man that would have travelled would have been a drover walking cattle and sheep to urban Britain. Turnpikes across the county were still being placed as late as 1830 when inter-urban railways were about to start. Stage and mail coaches with the associated hotel, stable yards and ostler mainly date from 1800 onwards. Therefore Montgomeryshire would have been one of the last areas to commence and finish with such services. There was little point in waiting for a stagecoach; there would not even have been a ghostly phaeton in most districts of that then very low income and isolated county.

The next transport development was the construction of the Montgomery canal. The full branch length was not completed until 1821. It remained a goods route with coal and lime coming in, and timber wool, some butter or cheese and grain leaving. The oak timber had naval importance, the grain trade collapsed with the repeal of 'The Corn Laws'. A fly barge operated from Rednal wharf to Newtown in the early 1850s. The wharf was 200 yards from Rednal station on the then Shrewsbury & Chester Railway. The service was soon withdrawn. The horse-drawn bus of the 1820s to 1890s would have been a large city business only, with truly zero potential in Montgomeryshire.

Various pony and traps carried people and many services worked to the railway stations. The other alternative was to walk. A pony and trap is seen in the centre of Kerry. The station at Glanmule was a distance of over a half-mile away.

David Pugh/Newtown Local History Group Collection

Jack Cookson was the founder of Cookson's Motor Services with buses after World War I. He learnt his skills as a chauffeur from 1905 onwards. He is seen driving Mr Powell's Humber in the Newtown area.

Mid-Wales Motorways Office

The county moved into the railway age with construction between 1859 and 1905. A horse-drawn support system developed from the stations to the surrounding villages and farms and this remained the pattern until the 1920s. There was no development of the omnibus. The horse-drawn omnibus and the horse-drawn tramways systems were features of large urban areas. Montgomeryshire had a share in this industry because of the quality of livestock husbandry. Many farmers carried extra brood mares and sold partially broken young horses to both urban transport and the cavalry. This trade became important enough to warrant the building of the horse repository close to the rail facilities of Newtown. This site was to become one of the largest bus depots ever used in the county after World War II. Experiments occurred with steam engines for omnibus and tram systems but there is no evidence of any such vehicle operating in this area. However, steam traction became important for hauling heavy timber and to support several lead mines. The County Council made use of the 1895 Light Railway Acts. The Llanyblodwel to Llangynog standard gauge line and the Welshpool to Llanfair narrow gauge line were constructed. The Cemmaes Road to Dinas Mawddwy line reopened as a light railway. All these were operated by steam locomotives within an agreement with the Cambrian Railways. Certain light railways in the expanding suburban areas were opened and most were powered by electricity. Many of the urban horse and steam railways started to be converted to electric power. This was to lead to British Electric Traction (BET). Also a Thomas Tilling had expanded with a horse-powered empire. This led to the two territorial dominant bus companies of the BET Group and the Thomas Tillling Group.

Early internal combustion engine buses started to become available from 1900 onwards. Crosville used the poor railway link between Ellesmere Port and Chester to set up a successful direct bus route. The Great Western Railway (GWR) did the same between Bridgnorth and Wolverhampton. The Cambrian Railways set up a bus link between Pwllheli and Nefyn. There were no pioneer developments within Montgomeryshire. The County Council considered further light railways in a report in 1917 with a view to ensuring men returning from the war had work. These were only ever at the suggestion stage but included the following:

To extend the Bishops Castle branch from Lydham through to Churchstoke and Montgomery Town.

To extend the Llanfyllin line to Llanwddyn. To extend the narrow gauge Welshpool to Llanfair line to Llanerfyl, Llangadfan and Y Foel.

To reopen the Van line for passengers and extend it to Llanidloes.

To re-build the failed line from Llanidloes to Llangurig.

To build a new railway from Machynlleth to Aberhosan with consideration of using the Corris narrow gauge.

World War I was fought and Montgomeryshire remained a county of horsepower fired by hay and rolled oats rather than petrol. There is still a haunting sadness in every part of Britain to see the list of young men and their deaths recorded on the local cenotaph. What now follows is a pattern repeated throughout rural Britain. Men were demobilized having acquired the skills of

The opening of the Welshpool & Llanfair Railway at Welshpool on 4th April, 1903. The Light Railways Acts passed in 1896 enabled local authorities to receive treasury funds to subsidize communications to isolated areas. The Cambrian managed the Welshpool to Llanfair, the Llanyblodwel to Llangynog and the re-opened Cemmaes to Dinas Mawwdwy branch. Col Stephens re-opened an independent line from Shrewsbury to Llanymynech that had a branch line to Criggion. Several of other planned light railways never materialized.

Powys County Council, Powysland Museum

The private wagonette was owned by and is parked outside the then Bear Hotel. The wagonette was used for the transport of passengers and luggage to and from the Newtown railway station. The picture is dated around 1912. *David Pugh/Newtown Local History Group Collection*

vehicle use either as a fitter or as a driver. They received a small gratuity. Some had some degree of war disability that made return to the quarry or farm difficult. At the same time, ex-War Department lorries came on to the market. These men took their opportunities starting small businesses and many were to prosper. Many would start to specialize in areas with larger villages. The business would soon become a garage or a haulage company or a bus company. Many from the isolated areas of Mid-Wales retained a multiple business with one or two vehicles only. This served as a delivery lorry, a hearse and livestock carrier. Soon this lorry would take cattle and sheep to the local market and then return to fit benches to take the farming family to the town. This pattern was still practised into the late 1930s. Therefore a pattern of bus services began. Soon the larger villages such as Kerry would justify a daily frequent service. Such a service from the centre of the village to the centre of Newtown or Welshpool removed custom from the railway branch lines. The family bus company knew their customers and such features as ticket issue and uniform were rare. Even Greenwich Mean Time hardly applied as the bus waited for the expected custom and did not leave town until the last local was counted back on. All the towns were compact without an internal bus service so most companies started from a rural parish working into town.

The War Department vehicles started to show signs of wear. The bus and coach industry had expanded rapidly in suburban areas and certainly contributed to further expansion such as ribbon development. Many of the more heavily populated villages started to have a frequent service causing rural workers to commute to factories, shops and offices. Aggressive territorial takeover occurred as the big brand names expanded. The bus manufacturers produced heavily-engineered single and double-deckers to meet the demand from the municipals replacing the trams and the provincials with their expansion. Such high capital cost could only be met by two-shift operation. Such capital and operating patterns could never be justified in upland Montgomeryshire. Crosville had started with a depot in Llanidloes that then moved to Llandrindod. They made some moves into the north of the county from Chester, Wrexham and Oswestry. There was a move down the Cambrian Coast from Llandudno down to Machynlleth. However they made few aggressive buy outs as happened along the North Wales Coast. The independents remained and they started to purchase some lighter buses such as second-hand Reos and new Fords and Chevrolets. The Bedford production from 1931 would answer the need for light coach and bus replacement until they dominated the market share by the late 1930s.

There is no evidence of several companies chasing each other along the main routes and ignoring any licensing guides in Montgomeryshire. A business just took a chance that there would be enough custom for even one small bus. This was not the case elsewhere and pressure led to regulation within the 1930 'Road Traffic Act'. The North West Commission based at Manchester was to issue licences for stage routes from that date. Maybe several of the small companies found the bureaucracy a burden and the appearance in front of the traffic court daunting. Several would start to struggle, as they could not update their bus. The situation led to the creation of Mid-Wales Motorways company in 1937 and

The wide use of the cycle for both work and leisure is rarely recorded. The photograph is outside Corfields of Newtown in the late 1940s and shows delivery of Phillips bicycles. These bikes were manufactured in a World War II shadow factory less than a mile from the shop between 1946 and 1958. The shop sold both Ariel motorbikes and radio aerials. Note the Austin van with the loudspeaker (Tannoy) available for hire for fetes, sports events etc.

David Pugh/Newtown Local History Group

Various bus/coach services boomed from 1930 to 1955. David was a student of Newtown High School in the early 1950s. The Mid-Wales Motorways Crossley taking them to see a Shakespeare play at the Stratford-upon-Avon Theatre suffered a mechanical failure in the Worcester area and the Newtown lads and the driver await assistance. A Midland Red bus arrived to take them on to Stratford and also for the return journey. *David Pugh*

this will be covered in detail. The GWR and Corris Railway had started several bus services in the 1920s from Welshpool and Machynlleth. GWR withdrew passenger services on the Kerry, the Mawddwy and the Llanfair branches in 1931. The GWR bus name transferred to Western Transport that also included the Wrexham tramway system and this merged into Crosville in 1933. Few long distance stagecoach routes developed and the only one traced in archives was Associated Motorways that had a Worcester, Llandrindod, Aberystwyth service via Llangurig. Excursion coaches and Saturday summer exchange coaches working through the county to the Cambrian resorts would have been an increasingly common sight.

World War II made an impact according to the geographical area and type of business. The extreme contraction took place with companies that had mainly excursion traffic. Mid-Wales companies suffered no contraction. Several Midland companies moved out into shadow factories to avoid the blitz. The need increased for both office and factory worked to have transport from the villages. The stage routes were therefore maintained and in some cases enhanced. Transport was available later for prisoners of war to work on farms. School contracts had to be maintained.

National and charity schools had a very patchy development before the 1870s Education Acts. The county filled in with all-age schools until up to 100 separate schools operated for children to be within walking distance of them. Secondary education with scholarship had a slow start but schools were available in the larger towns that now have the six comprehensive schools. This led to both rail season tickets and school bus contracts from 1920 onwards. The 1944 Education Act would raise the school leaving age to 15 with secondary education for all. Depopulation and the demise of the local all-age school would lead to the closure of many of the smaller schools. It was therefore necessary to have a smaller bus/taxi service for primary schools and a large bus delivery system to the towns. The school contract soon became, and remains, the most important income for a local bus company.

The decade 1945 to 1955 was the boom period. There were still only a few cars and petrol rationing continued after the war. Many were to receive better wages with more free time and paid holidays. Fares were cheap, the buses and coaches had excellent occupancy so companies such as Mid-Wales Motorways paid good wages and profit levels were sufficient for capital renewal. It is certain that many did not appreciate the huge problems that would soon arrive. The British Transport Commission (BTC), in 1948, took over railways, canals, civilian airways and road haulage. The bus industry was in an uncertain period as the BTC extended negotiations with companies outside the Tilling and BET group and then with the two large companies. Mid-Wales Motorways was one of the larger of the independents considered. It was not purchased and this was considered with some regret as price transfer was considered to be very good.

The use of the private car started to expand relentlessly. Bus services were not frequent in such rural areas as Montgomeryshire. A farmer would buy a dual-purpose vehicle. The commonest must have been the A40 van or pick-up or the Morris Minor equivalent. There is no doubt that car use widened rural work and culture with the flexibility of door-to-door transit and no time restrictions.

One farmer would acquire a vehicle and he would pass on the driving skill to his wife, his brothers and sisters, the children and friends. It was of such value that the area would soon be full of second-hand and new vehicles. There were both rail and bus strikes in the 1950s. This was a disaster because the close knit community offered lifts to market for the older people and continued to do so when the service was restored. The use of one-man operation and the use of second-hand buses cascaded down from the big companies helped survival in the rapidly shrinking market. The first subsidy of rebates on fuel helped the larger state and private companies. The BTC was abolished in 1962. The bus companies had moved within a decade from high occupancy and low fares to fewer passengers with higher fares to attempt to maintain income. The high occupancy routes could no longer subsidize the less frequent outlying routes. The growth of TV in the home led to a collapse of market town cinema trade and this caused the withdrawal of virtually every evening service. The stage route system for rural buses was now grim.

Consideration was given to special rural subsidies and the GPO was asked to investigate dual use of delivery vehicles. Spare capacity on certain school buses could also be used for stage fares. The minibus use increased but a company often needed a larger bus for school or factory work so that the mid-morning, mid-afternoon service would often be seen with a handful of passengers in a 40 seat-plus bus.

The motorway network expanded in the 1960s increasing the use of long distance coaches. The few coaches operating on several days per week to Cardiff, Liverpool, Cheltenham and Bangor struggled to survive as they travelled across the county with no motorway. Many rail lines shut between 1962 and 1965. The village stations closed on the remaining through line leaving just four stations in the county Machynlleth, Caersws, Newtown and Welshpool. (Dyfi Junction is also within the county but is an exchange station with only a few passengers boarding or leaving for Glandyfi). A splendid effort was made in the niche market of tours both within the British Isles and on the continent. This would assist viability during the 1970s/1980s and still remains an important section of business for several companies.

Political interference had been minimal up to the late 1960s as much legislation governed safety and control of standards. Change became constant swinging from one political concept of planning to the opposite of deregulation. Once again the Mid-Wales independents continued to struggle on in their own way as they represented a minute turnover of the UK bus industry. Barbara Castle took on her remit for transport with much energy. First of all, the Passenger Transport Executives were set up in major urban areas. Then the National Bus Company was formed in January 1969 and North Wales and much of Central Wales was within the Crosville area that also combined with Ribble (Lancashire). The County Councils could arrange a subsidy. Health and Safety Acts placed the cab of the vehicle as a workplace. An operator had to have a licence and a syllabus with examination levels evolved. The fitting of a tachograph became necessary. Yet various community schemes with minibuses and volunteer drivers were allowed from 1978. Then the pendulum was to swing with the election of Mrs Thatcher and the Conservatives. Company deregulation and the winding up of the National Bus Company followed. In urban areas, fierce competition and some failure occurred. Some aspects of the work of Mr Nicholas Ridley, the Transport Minister around 1984, may not look well in retrospect.

He became a zealot rather than a pragmatist. Certain companies may have been 'asset stripped' for the 'real estate' value of the central bus station. Also orders for new buses virtually ceased for several years and this may have contributed to the demise of the UK bus manufacturing industry. It was a lottery if men were re-employed with similar conditions of work and pension continuation. No fierce battles for routes took place in Powys. Soon the problem of social need for rural services led to the concept of counties asking companies for a competitive tender for individual routes. This would lead to the concept of Bws Powys, Bws Gwynedd, Shropshire Bus etc.

The Welsh Assembly replaced the Welsh Office in the late 1990s and much effort has been made to enhance public transport. Pensioners can apply for a free pass and this is of great value if one lives in Newport or Cardiff but cannot be widely used in Montgomeryshire. Help has been given with low floor loading buses to increase access for those with mobility problems. One pensioner from Colwyn Bay arranged with his assembly member that he could travel the length of Wales to Cardiff on stage routes. He arrived for the promised free lunch after three days' travel. The map routes for Montgomeryshire timetables now show that most villages have a service. It looks very comprehensive until studied. It can only exist because of Powys County Council support. Most villages have a minimal service in the morning and afternoon, some still only operate on market days. Some services are school/college days only. There are virtually no services even within towns after 6.00 pm. The stage routes remain a rural social service or town services to reduce congestion that must look like open space compared with Cardiff or London. The current situation would never tempt someone to give up their car.

This sets the rural scene. The 1920s saw the territorial expansion of BET and the Tilling Group. Currently Arriva Midlands North work some routes in the Severn Valley and the border, Arriva Cymru operate in the western area and the Arriva Cymru/Wales operates the train service. It poses the question of why the need for deregulation if large companies evolve again. Maybe there is a need for large operating companies as if it is almost within the genetic make up of the industry. Smaller independents have always found a living within certain needs throughout the history of the bus industry. This history for Montgomeryshire now follows demonstrating how skill, enterprise and hard work enables an independent bus company to trade and survive in such difficult territory.

WELSHPOOL—NEWTOWN via BERRIEW

	Daily.				Sunday.	
	A.M.	P.M.	P.M	P.M. *Saturdays only.*	P.M.	P.M
WELSHPOOL *dep.*	10 0	2 15	5 35	10 10	3 15	8 15
Coedydinas ...	10 6	2 21	5 41	10 16	3 21	8 21
Llwynderw...	10 11	2 26	5 46	10 21	3 26	8 26
Horse Shoe...	10 17	2 32	5 52	10 27	3 32	8 32
Berriew ...	10 25	2 40	6 0	10 35	3 40	8 40
Revel ...	10 33	2 48	6 8	10 43	3 48	8 48
Garthmyl ...	10 38	2 53	6 13	10 48	3 53	8 53
Halfway ...	10 43	2 58	6 18	10 53	3 58	8 58
Abermule ...	10 53	3 8	6 28	11 3	4 8	9 8
Bettws Turning ...	11 0	3 15	6 35	11 10	4 15	9 15
NEWTOWN *arr.*	11 10	3 25	6 45	11 20	4 25	9 25

LIST OF FARES.

	s. d.		s. d.
NEWTOWN ...	—	WELSHPOOL ...	—
Bettws Turning ...	0 3	Coedydinas Cottages	0 2
Abermule ...	0 6	Horse Shoe ...	0 6
Halfway ...	0 9	Berriew ...	0 8
Gathmyl ...	0 11	Revel... ...	0 8
Revel... ...	1 1	Garthmyl ...	0 10
Berriew ...	1 1	Halfway ...	1 0
Horse Shoe ...	1 3	Abermule ...	1 3
Coedydinas Cottages	1 7	Bettws Turning ...	1 6
WELSHPOOL ...	1 9	NEWTOWN ...	1 9

Special Return Fare.—Newtown to Welshpool (or vice versa) 2/-.

NEWTOWN—WELSHPOOL Via MONTGOMERY, CHURCHSTOKE and CHIRBURY

	Daily, except Sunday.	*Mondays only.*	*Daily, except Sunday & Monday*	*Mondays only*	Sunday.	
	A.M.	P.M.	P.M.	P.M.	P.M.	P.M.
NEWTOWN *dep.*	8 30	2 0	3 0		1 0	5 40
Bettws Turning ..	8 40	2 10	3 10		1 10	5 50
Abermule ...	8 47	2 17	3 17		1 17	5 57
Halfway ...	8 55	2 25	3 25		1 25	6 5
Garthmyl, Nag's Hd.	9 0	2 30	3 30		1 30	6 10
Caerhowel Bridge ..	9 4	2 34	3 34		1 34	6 14
Montgomery ...	9 14	2 44	3 44	4 35	1 44	6 24
Blue Bell ...	9 26	2 56	3 56		1 56	6 36
Churchstoke ...	9 32	3 2	4 2		2 2	6 42
Chirbury ...	9 44	3 14	4 14	4 45	2 14	6 54
Forden ...	9 55	3 25	4 25	4 56	2 25	7 5
Cilkewydd ...	9 59	3 29	4 29	5 0	2 29	7 9
Coedydinas Cott. ...	10 3	3 33	4 33	5 4	2 33	7 13
WELSHPOOL *arr.*	10 9	3 39	4 39	5 10	2 39	7 19

LIST OF FARES.

	s. d.		s. d.
NEWTOWN ...	—	WELSHPOOL ...	—
Bettws Turning ...	0 3	Coedydinas Cottages	0 2
Abermule ...	0 6	Cilkewydd ...	0 4
Halfway ...	0 9	Forden ...	0 6
Garthmyl, Nag's Hd.	0 11	Chirbury ...	0 10
Caerhowel Bridge ..	1 1	Churchstoke...	1 2
Montgomery ...	1 4	Blue Bell ...	1 4
Blue Bell ...	1 7	Montgomery ...	1 2
Churchstoke ...	1 9	Caerhowel Bridge	1 5
Chirbury ...	1 8	Garthmyl, Nag's Hd.	1 7
Forden ...	2 0	Halfway ...	1 9
Cilkewydd ...	2 2	Abermule ...	2 0
Coedydinas Cottages	2 4	Bettws Turning ...	2 3
WELSHPOOL ...	2 6	NEWTOWN ...	2 6

The direct bus route from Newtown to Welshpool and the loop route are both shown on this map. The Great Western Railway closed both the Kerry and Llanfair branches to passengers in 1931 due to bus competition. The largest village between Newtown and Welshpool is Berriew. The longer 'loop' route connected Montgomery town, Churchstoke and Chirbury (Shropshire) to public transport. Montgomery railway station was over a mile away from the town.

Chapter Two

Mid-Wales Motorways of Newtown

School contracts commenced in the late 1920s until they now dominate the turnover of many local companies. Six chapters will each therefore cover the companies and services that have arisen to service the six towns (Llanfair Caereinion, Llanfyllin, Llanidloes, Machynlleth, Newtown and Welshpool) that have a comprehensive (high) school. This is not an exact division. The six towns were also the focal point of past and current stage routes. This first Newtown chapter is broken into nine subsections. The following chapter looks at other companies of Newtown. There are several reasons for this division. The first was that Newtown was the head office for Mid-Wales Motorways (MWM). No book on this topic is possible without considering the major impact of the now historic Mid-Wales Motorways or Crosville companies. Their roots extended deeply into the fabric of the local bus industry in past decades. Newtown is the largest town in the area. It therefore had and retains a large number of stage routes including the largest town service in Powys. It is, as yet, the only town with a specific bus station with bays in Montgomeryshire as opposed to allocated bus stops within the streets or town parks.

Newtown is an old town for it was a planned settlement founded by Edward 1st with a Charter around 1279. It replaced the town and fortress of Dolforwyn near Abermule after the defeat of Llewelyn. The 'Nova Villa' was built by a ford to cross the Severn around the community of Llanfair-yng-Nghedewain. Cedewain was an area of an autonomous lordship and the name is still used in the area as well as for the church deanery. The town prospered and became a natural centre for the wool trade. Robert Owen was a Newtown man famous as a socialist philospher and founder of the concept of co-operation in the early 19th century. The town became a major centre for wool manufacture based on waterwheel power but declined as steam power moved the industry to the West Riding of Yorkshire.

The canal terminus arrived around 1820 and operated (just) until the early 1940s. The railways arrived from 1859 and early 1860s with three different companies (Llanidloes & Newtown, Newtown & Machynlleth and Newtown & Oswestry) prior to the formation of the Cambrian Railways. Pryce Jones pioneered the concept of mail order for Welsh flannel and then other goods in the 1870s and this generated much rail traffic.

A very slow urban and rural decline became a feature of Mid-Wales. The problem was faced in the early 1960s with a concept of a linear town between Newtown and Caersws with a population of 70,000. This was diluted with the foundation of 'The Development Board for Rural Wales'. The town commenced an expansion from around 6,000 to the current 13,000 people. Expansion with factories, offices, housing and improved infrastructure took place throughout the region. Newtown is now the largest community in Powys. It has major administrative work, distribution, and manufacturing facilities with all the extra services that follow. These tend to dominate the tourist potential. The town has several important heritage buildings, several museums and the main

This Dennis became part of the MWM fleet in 1937 when William Tudor of Welshpool merged into the new company. This coach was the luxury vehicle of the fleet having a radio. FW 4875 was used with three Dennis units transferred by the War Department to the company in 1942 to ensure workers were delivered to the expanding shadow factories. The FW registration immediately gave this coach the ironic nickname of Focke-Wulf. *David Hughes Collection*

Dennis AEP 517 was purchased new in late 1945 as a priority order. Displaced persons from Eastern Europe were moved to Tonfannau ex-army camp near Tywyn.This bus then dispersed these people to sites around the UK ready to integrate them into the community. Bill collected the bus from the factory at Guilford. He was used to older Dennis buses with heavy flywheels and crash boxes and made a bit of a hash of the first few yards with a diesel with synchromesh box. *David Hughes Collection*

art gallery for the area. The surrounding villages have much attraction and two examples are Kerry with the Ridgeway and Tregynon with Gregynog Hall. The town justifies the most frequent bus town service in the area.

Vesting day, May 1937

Seventeen years had passed since the end of World War I when many men started their bus company. The early buses of the 1920s were often former lorries with a shared body. By 1930, too many buses were chasing too few customers and bus regulations were introduced in 1930. The British bus industry concentrated supply to the municipals such as Cardiff Corporation and inter-town companies (the provincials) such as Crosville as need expanded. Also, tramway systems were not being renewed. A gap was left in many rural areas for small rural independents. They neither needed nor could afford the sturdily built British bus and imports such as Reo (USA), Fiat (Italy) etc. filled the gap. One of the most successful was the General Motors Chevrolet. General Motors observed this and introduced the light British made Bedford PSV units in 1931 and had achieved 70 per cent of the light bus market by 1939. The rural bus became a tremendous success.

Bill Cross was one of the sons of R. Alfred Cross. Bill was born in Canada. Dad was related, by marriage, to the Cooksons of Newtown who had both a garage and bus interests. Alfred was asked to return to Wales to take on management of the bus section. Bill's father found the bus section to be chaotic. He called a meeting of all the local owners. Such income as school contracts had become so competitive that there was no margin for capital renewal. It was decided to amalgamate, with each owner having shares. In some ways, it was an owner's co-operative and each took their turn as chair. Bill thinks that Edward Neale was the first. This led to the creation of the company called Mid-Wales Motorways and a rational system started to develop.

A list of some of those who joined now follows:

John Cookson owned four garages in the Newtown area. He had a Leyland, a Karrier, three 14-seat Chevrolets and two Bedfords.

Les Jones was another Newtown company. He was nicknamed Bon-bon as his wife kept a sweet shop. His contribution was two 14-seat vehicles.

Edward Neale of Severn Motors had a rare collection, most of which had ceased to function. There was an AEC, an AJS better known for motorcycles and a Dennis. One vehicle had detachable seats so it was used to take livestock to market and then it would return for a hose-out before collecting passengers.

Mr Tudor of Welshpool brought in a 32 seat Dennis Lancet with radio plus other less luxurious buses.

A Mr Jenkins of Llanidloes contributed two small buses that were used on the Staylittle run.

Trevor Jones of Llangurig came in with two buses.

A Mr Weaver had several 14-seaters that worked to Mochdre.

Ernie Davies from Bettws brought in a Vulcan Duchess and a Vulcan Duke.

Edward Evans from New Mills brought in a luxury parlour coach and two other buses.

'Bon-bon Bluebird' was one of the coaches owned by Les Jones of Newtown prior to joining Mid-Wales Motorways in 1937. The family also kept a sweet shop, hence bon-bon. The name Bluebird is often associated with speed but was also a well-known brand of toffee. The bus may be Guy EP 4701. *Eddie Francis and Mid-Wales Motorways*

The system of cascading down buses from other companies also gave trade between the independents. EP 8402, new to MWM, was sold to Silver Star and is seen parked in Caernarfon Square. *Eddie Francis and Mid-Wales Motorways*

The initial amalgamation was deemed successful and several other companies joined in before the outbreak of World War II and the last company came into the company in 1945. Mr Williams of Halfway House came in with two buses. J.F. Pryce sold both his bus and his Bwlch-y-ffridd route to the company in 1938. Mid-Wales Motorways purchased both the buses and the Four Crosses to Shrewsbury route from Coopers of Oakengates in 1938. Coopers could then concentrate on their core business in what is now the Telford area. Mr Bunce of Worthen also came in with two buses retaining his own main business of coal haulage. This added the Worthen Motors with the important Montgomery to Shrewsbury route in 1945. The David John Arthur fleet joined from Llanerfyl towards the end of the war with two buses and the Llanfair depot was created.

At one point there were over 70 vehicles in the yards and most were obsolete. A list has been found in the Omnibus Society archives and some details now follow:

Karrier & Star Flier from Cookson's. Maudslay from Evans New Mills. Vulcan & Reo from Coopers. TSM (revamped Tilling Stevens) from Jones, Llangurig. General Motors Coach from Williams Halfway House. AJS Pilot from Neales Newtown. Bean from Jones Llangurig. Two Vulcans from Davies Bettws. The others on the list were Chevrolets, Bedfords, Dennis units, Guys and Leylands.

The early garage was on the New Road which became very restricted as the power station was built. The company moved to the Old Church Garage of John Cookson at Skinner Street beside the tannery. The attached house became the office. It adjoined the site next to St Mary's Church.

Bill joined the company in 1937 as a trainee mechanic at the age of fourteen. He could only be a mechanic until 17 when he was entitled to drive the 14-seater. Bill joined the RAF for the duration of the war and came back to MWM from 1945 to 1950 until he set up his own garage business at Dulas in partnership with Fred Worrall.

The company started to rationalize with more modern units. Five Daimlers were purchased from the Kent Road Car Company. The contract was obtained for taking local workers to the construction of the Marchweil Army camp as re-armament gained pace before the outbreak of war. New 28 hp 27-seat Bedfords were purchased and four 5-cylinder Gardner diesel Guys joined the fleet. The company immediately expanded Sunday school and Saturday excursions business with the better buses.

Bill is one of many who served in World War II. No one who worked for the company during the war can now be located. Bus regulations were complex and certain changes came about but Bill was uncertain of the dates. Certainly a driver only could operate a 14-seater but a conductor was also required on board for fare collection once capacity was over 20 passengers. The rules were relaxed during the war period. Pick up points were also licensed. The Crosville Company had the licence from Newtown to Llanidloes so MWM could only drive along the road but was not allowed to collect anyone. The amalgamation of the smaller companies into MWM gave far greater flexibility.

A five-cylinder Gardner diesel engine powered the Guy EP 9502. These had been scaled down from a six-cylinder design to give greater fuel economy during the war and post-war fuel shortages. They were slow with a heavy chassis and coach body. *David Hughes Collection*

The company had one Austin purchased soon after the war. The body had been placed on a lorry chassis so the vehicle had hard springs and a hard ride. *David Hughes Collection*

Bill reflects on several post-war duties. He travelled down to Guildford to the Dennis works with Ted Evans soon after demobilization. Two new Lancets had been allocated to the company; one with a discount as Dennis wanted a full operational report on the new design to operate in an area with many gradients. The seating capacity of this was around 36 passengers. The duty was to Tonfannau near Tywyn. The camp was used for the initial housing of displaced persons from Eastern Europe. The contract was to disperse these people to smaller units around Britain. Bill would therefore leave Newtown at 4.00 am to be at Tonfannau at 6.00 am. It would only be then that he would know the destination. Signposting had not been reinstated from the war. The first journey was to Barnards Castle in Durham. Every journey had several stops at church halls etc. so the passengers could have a visit to the lavatories and take refreshments. He drove the Dennis to every corner of England over the next six months. Most deliveries were to ex-RAF camps. Bill would often sleep in the guard's room and then drive back to Newtown the following day in an empty coach with solitude after the Polish or Ukrainian chatter. The following morning, Bill was out at 4.00 am again and 14 hours later, he could be anywhere from Hastings to Scarborough.

Bill recalled that in 1947 and 1948 the company won the tender for the Newtown Joint Sunday School trip to Aberystwyth. The railway company usually had such business. All the company coaches had to be used and the buses were on the normal stage routes for that day. Drivers and coaches were hired in from such companies as Salopia of Whitchurch and Hampsons of Oswestry.

Bill followed the convoy in a van with a full set of tools in case of a breakdown. The coaches all lined up on New Road outside St David's church and made up a magnificent sight before departure. In 1948, 27 coaches were used for over 700 pupils and parents. The morning run was via Llanidloes and Ponterwyd and the afternoon return via Machynlleth and Llanbrynmair. Excursion rights given by the traffic commissioners determined the route for all companies.

The most important stage route was Newtown to Welshpool, either direct or via Montgomery. The traffic commissioners blocked the direct route to Shrewsbury until after Bill had left the company. It was possible to travel via Chirbury and Worthen or from Four Crosses via Crew Green. The buses were not allowed to pick up or put down close to Shrewsbury as the urban stops were allocated to Midland Red.

Bill hopes the pre-war account has some accuracy, as he is recalling his time as a teenager over 65 years ago. He has selected some photographs from the David Hughes collection.

Henry Cookson recalls Uncle Jack

Henry was born in 1923. Grandfather was the last coachman at Glansevern House. Glansevern Gardens have been restored and are open to the public. He had four sons. Uncle John (known as Jack in the family) transferred grandfather's skill to become a chauffeur to a Newtown solicitor who was also

The card postmark (dated 1908 at Garthmyl Post Office) shows uncle 'Jack Cookson' with a motorbike and two cars. Uncle was then chauffeur/mechanic for Mr Powell, a Newtown solicitor and a Director of the Humber Motor Company. *Henry Cookson, Berriew*

Cookson's Motor Services at the Halfway shop near Garthmyl on the service from Newtown to Welshpool. Henry believes uncle is one of the men. He cannot recall the bus make but dates the picture around 1924 because the bus has solid tyres. *Henry Cookson, Berriew*

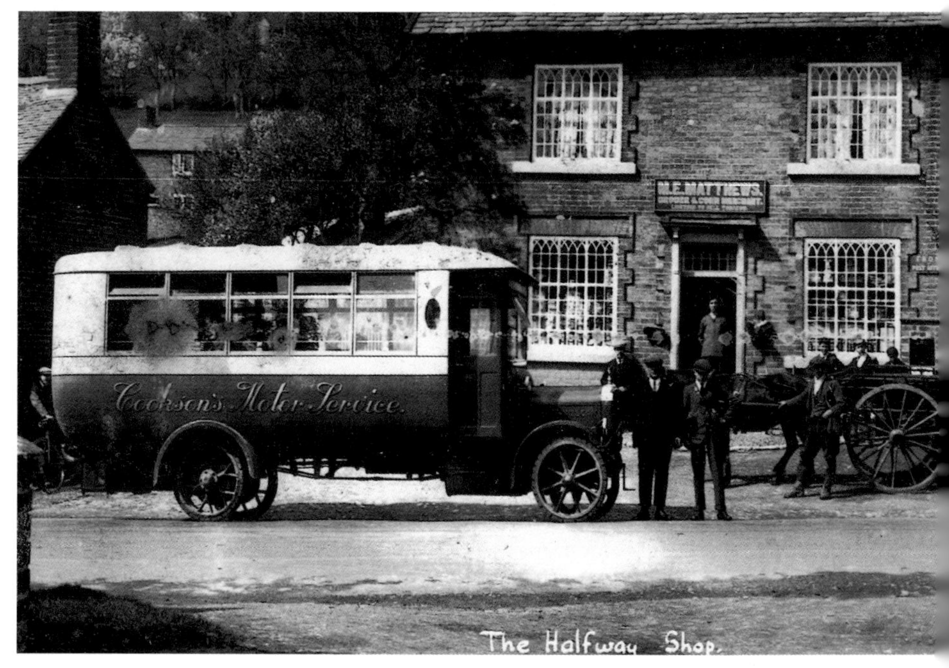

MID WALES MOTORWAYS
NEWTOWN
EP 7520
AAY 588
VJ 9128

The Dodge undergoes repair. The only Dodge came from either Davies of Bettws (Omnibus Society list) or Evans of New Mills (local recall). Dodge imported and then assembled vehicles at Kew. The coach had a six-cylinder 23 hp engine and the aim was to dent the dominance of Bedford in the light coach market. *Omnibus Society*

The Dennis half-cab is at the Gravel bus park. The starting handle would indicate that it was a petrol engine unit. The destination on the front is Welshpool. The heavier half-cabs were employed on the trunk roads. No one can make out the half front of the vehicle in the background. *Omnibus Society*

spinster sister of Dad, was the conductress. After 1937, the buses started at New Mills and Llanfair depots.

Ernie Davies had survived a mustard attack during World War I and his lungs were fragile. Smoking aggravated the situation. The Bettws buses were now parked in Cookson's yard. Dad became a shareholder and staff member. The house in Newtown had a very large garden and Walter had to look after a very large vegetable plot. The growing of vegetables within gardens and allotments was vital to increase food availability.

Walter cannot recollect the full details of restrictions and changes during the war period. Many stage routes continued and such services were packed. Virtually all excursions and leisure travel ceased. There were many more people travelling in from the outlying villages to assist wartime production. Accles & Pollock had a shadow factory. Price Brothers started making precision aircraft parts. Military clothing was made at both Pryce Jones and Cymric Mills. The Admiralty moved a victualling office to the town. There was a large army camp on the site of the current High School, an Italian prisoner of war camp at Dulas and a Land Army camp at Caersws. All these generated extra work for the company. There were several buses deployed on taking workers to the new Ordnance factory at Marchweil near Wrexham. Crosville deployed many buses from North Wales and Cheshire to supply staff for this essential factory. The company would have had priority for fuel to maintain such services. There may have been a limited stop policy of one pick-up/set down point in the central area of the villages. The central point for Newtown was the Gravel Park. The company changed from a male-dominated company to one employing women for every duty. Most had to move on when the men who had served in the war were guaranteed a return work place. Dad was not even fit enough to join the Home Guard but he had to do one night shift every week on the switchboard of the police station. Tragedy occurred when John, the older brother of Audrey and Walter, was killed in Normandy about three weeks after D-Day. Walter recalls a journey to Worcester with Dad and Mr Neale to inspect and collect a bus. The company had been issued with a special permit to take the car to Worcester. The car was stopped for a check and Ernie was admonished for taking Walter for a day out.

Walter left school in 1944 and started work on a GPO bicycle as a telegram boy. He was transferred to the telephone section and his duties would be that of a linesman. However, he would help the bus company at weekends and acquired both a driver and a conductor's licence. The company moved the bus depot from the area of St Mary's to the horse repository by the cattle market soon after the war. Walter recalls stripping out the stables and some of the fine oak divisions were sold to one of the schools for woodwork. The place was cleaned out as it had been used as a strategic wheat grain store during the war. Pits were made for inspection, electricity installed and the floors were covered in concrete so most buses could be stored undercover. The same site is still the Newtown depot for the successor 'Mid Wales Travel' although there is pressure for alternative developments. Walter's duties would be mainly excursion trips. Some weekends would see every bus on duty. Priority for extra work and overtime was always given to the full time staff so Walter was the last reserve.

The entry to Old Church Yard was via the narrow part of Skinner Street by the fellmongers skin yard. The Bedford WTB squeezes through with close observation from the conductress. It may be Cis Kinsey of Kerry. Access and site restriction prevented any development of a bus station at the main depot so passengers waited 200 yards away at the Gravel. *Omnibus Society*

VE 5551 is one of the Daimlers CF6s purchased soon after the new company was created It is ex-Burwell & District. EP 6595 is ex-Neales of Newtown. EP 8317 is a war delivery Bedford OWB and this was the only new light wartime bus when there was very limited supply. The driver is likely to be Roy Owen. *Omnibus Society*

One duty would be the conductor on the Cardiff run at peak weekends. He once took over £200 in fares as the two coaches were packed all the way. Most work was as a conductor rather than a driver.

Dad died around 1967. He had struggled with ill health and his duties were within the office on working timetables, service schedules etc. before he retired. The company was making a profit until petrol rationing ceased and the use of the car expanded rapidly. There were up to 80 buses held at Newtown, Llanfair, Llanidloes, Welshpool and Worthen. Dad was a Director during the period from 1953 when decline started. Board meetings became acrimonious and a solicitor was required at each meeting. The company Secretary was Sidney Griffiths and he worked hard to rationalize change. Certainly Dad found changes stressful due to his ill health.

Walter ceased any connection with the company by 1960 when telephone duties required much weekend work and standby. He could not get a house when first married around 1956. He and his new wife commenced married life in a caravan parked in the bus yard. He paid a nominal rent and was asked to take any late phone calls. One was received from a driver on a return from a Blackpool excursion. The line was not clear and Walter interpreted the following. 'I have lumbago and my back is going, may not make it but will struggle to Oswestry'. Walter found his father and they both set off to Oswestry so Walter could drive the coach back. They found the coach with a very fit driver who asked 'Where is the spare bus'. The message had been that the engine was lumbering and the big ends going! Anyhow the coach limped back to Newtown.

Ernie Davies is remembered by some of the now older people as a real gentleman with the trait of extreme honesty. Both Walter and Audrey recall this trait. Dad could not understand that a passenger would try to avoid payment or some conductors would try to slip a few coins into their own pockets. He was an idealist in a world where there would have been no need for ticket inspectors.

Ivy Evans: A long career with Mid-Wales Motorways

Edward Evans was the late uncle of Ivy. He was the third child of David and Eleanor Evans. David was a corn merchant. Edward was born in 1886 and started business as a grocer/general dealer at the stores at New Mills. Somewhere around 1910, he started a service of pony and trap to Welshpool with a journey time of 2½ hours and a return fare of 1s. He already was helping to deliver goods for his father with a donkey and cart. Edward, often known as Ned, purchased a Ford van and started the local garage in 1919. A lorry was purchased for livestock and general goods in 1921. Then, around 1923, he purchased a utility 12-seat bus. The seats could be taken out so it was also a hearse, or a bread van or livestock feed delivery van. The bus service was a success and soon justified vehicles solely for public transport. The company traded as Rhiew Valley Motor Services. He maintained two light buses as these could be operated as driver only. He then purchased a 28-seat coach that would

Right: The uncle of Ivy, Edward Evans, started a bus business at New Mills after World War I. The company traded as Rhiew Valley Motor Services. Edward joined the Mid-Wales grouping in 1937. The picture dates from the late 1940s when he was a Director of the company.

Ivy Evans, Berriew

Below: Ivy receives an inscribed goblet from John Griffith, Managing Director of MWM to mark 40 years' service to the company.

The County Times, September 1986

have required a conductor for stage fare operation. The profit of such an enterprise without regulation soon attracted more operators so that profit had become marginal by 1935. He therefore took the opportunity to put his share into Mid-Wales Motorways in 1937. Edward died at the age of 79 in 1965.

Ivy passed the scholarship and attended Newtown Girls Grammar School from September 1939. The mode of transport was uncle's bus. Ivy left school in July 1944 and worked for two years for the Admiralty who had a victualling office in Newtown. She still came to work on the same bus except for the school holidays when she cycled. The Admiralty moved this victualling service back to the ports once the danger of bombing had ceased so Ivy was facing redundancy. Uncle offered Ivy the chance to start as a bus conductress for three days per week. The bus route was Adfa to Newtown plus Bwlch-y-ffridd and Aberhafesb on Tuesdays and Saturdays. Soon work became three days per week on the bus and three days in the office at Newtown. Then the duties became mainly within the office as the junior with such duties as checking tickets, taking in parcels for village delivery and checking out parcels for collection. The bus companies played a vital role in parcel delivery during and immediately after the war. Ivy took on the senior duties of book keeping, wages and cashier's duties in the early 1950s. At the peak of activity, the company had over 100 staff at the various depots. Most services still had conductors as well as drivers. The company had fitters, cleaners, ticket-inspectors, clerical staff and even a lady cook at Newtown.

There were four Directors from 1937 until 1963. They were uncle Edward Evans, J.S. Neale of Newtown, Ernie Davies of Bettws and Mr Ernest Williams of Halfway House. They purchased and supervised the move to the horse repository in 1947/48. The Old Church Yard site was rented to Shukers as an Agricultural Engineering Premise. The direct route to Shrewsbury via Welshpool was licensed to the company with much opposition in 1949. They all retired due to trading difficulties except for Mr Neale. The restructured company was called Mid-Wales Motorways 1963 and that registration stands to this day. Mr Neale was Managing Director of the new company for only a few months before his sudden death. Four former employees now took on the company. Mr Sidney Griffiths, the ex-company Secretary became Managing Director, Reg Meddins became traffic manager and two drivers, Mr Aneurin Jones and Mr Iorwerth Oliver, made up the Board. They immediately faced the problems caused by increasing car ownership, higher fuel prices and wages but declining number of passengers. Depots had already closed, many licences were surrendered and many villages were left without public transport. The horse repository was sold and leased back.

Sidney Griffith retired in 1978 and his son, John, returned from London. John arranged many more day trips, short breaks and holidays both within the British Isles and on the continent. In April 1987, the company celebrated 50 years of trading. A lovely party was held at the Elephant, a local hotel, with staff members that were on the current payroll and many former employees and relatives of the founders. The company was sold to D.J. Evans and Sons of Penrhyncoch, Aberystwyth in 1988. The company retains the Newtown depot and trades as Mid Wales Travel. Ivy continued to work giving clerical support

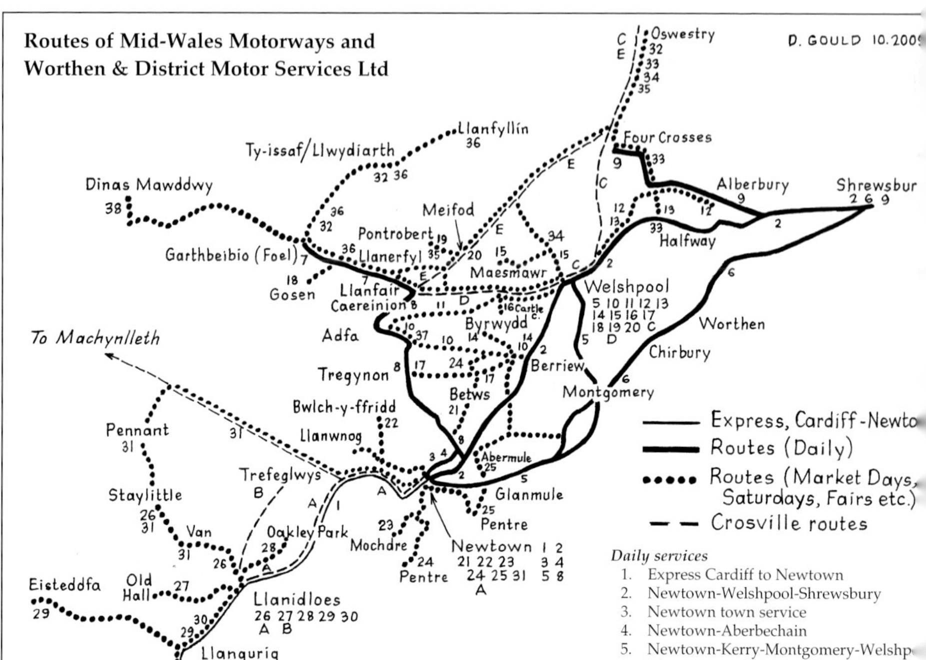

Daily services

1. Express Cardiff to Newtown
2. Newtown-Welshpool-Shrewsbury
3. Newtown town service
4. Newtown-Aberbechain
5. Newtown-Kerry-Montgomery-Welshpool
6. Montgomery-Chirbury-Shrewsbury
7. Garthbeibio (Foel) -Llanfair Caereinion
8. Llanfair Caereinion-Newtown
9. Four Crosses-Shrewsbury

Services on Market Day, Saturday, Fairs, etc

10. Adfa-Berriew-Welshpool
11. New Mills-Byrwydd-Golfa-Welshpool
12. Alderbury-Welshpool
13. Halfway-Winnington-Welshpool
14. Byrwydd-Berriew-Welshpool
15. Maesmawr-Welshpool
16. Castle Caereinion-Welshpool
17. Tregynon-Betws-Brooks-Welshpool
18. Gosen-Llanerfyl-Welshpool
19. Pontrobert-Welshpool
20. Meifod-Welshpool
21. Betws-Blackhouse-Newtown
22. Bwlch-y-ffridd-Newtown
23. Mochdre-Pentre-Newtown
24. Pentre Llifior-Brooks-Newtown
25. Abermule-Glanmule-Pentre-Newtown
26. Staylittle-Van-Llanidloes
27. Old Hall-Llanidloes
28. Oakley Park-Llanidloes
29. Eisteddfa-Llangurig-Llanidloes
30. Llanidloes-Llangurig-Rhayader (with fair day-only extra to Elan Valley)
31. Van-Staylittle-Penneant-Newtown
32. Ty-issaf-Llwydiarth-Oswestry
33. Halfway House-Oswestry
34. Pentrebeirdd-Oswestry
35. Pontrobert-Oswestry
36. Llanerfyl-Llanfyllin
37. New Mills-Llanfair Caereinion
38. Llanerfyl-Dinas Mawddwy

This map acts as a guide only as the River Severn flood of 1960 destroyed much material at the MWM Severn Square office at Newtown.

The Cardiff express was daily in the summer months, otherwise three days per week.
The Newtown-Welshpool-Shrewsbury service operated up to eight to 10 times, and three times on Sunday.
Llanfair Caereinion-Newtwon had one service operating at workmen's times on weekdays plus extras on Tuesdays and Saturdays.

Market Day Services
Some services operated on market day and Saturdays usuch as Newtown-Mochdre, others were market day only such as Pontrobert-Oswestry and others Saturday only such as Oakley Park-Llanidloes. Others were monthly fair days only, or twice per year, such as Llanerfyl-Dinas Mawddwy. Some, such as the Elan Valley Wednesday fair day-only had been withdrawn during World war II and recommenced in 1946. It was withdrawn once more in the early 1950s.

MWM routes at 1951 from a project by John Griffiths (*see page 41*).

The labour force at MWM had halved since a peak in the early 1950s. Some of the staff of the late 1950s is seen in front of the Cardiff Express Daimler at the Newtown yard. From left to right are: Reg Meddins and Iorwerth Oliver (Iori) both drivers and both became working Directors of Mid-Wales Motorways 1963, Neil Atkinson (apprentice) stands in the coach behind Cyril Hamer (driver) of Montgomery, Reg Evans (driver) of Tregynon stands beside Frank of Birmingham. Frank was a trained tool setter and he was excellent on any lathe work. *Geoff Williams, Kerry*

Both local agricultural merchants and local branches of the farmers unions would often arrange a visit to one of the National Compounders Experimental Farms. This one was to the British Oil and Cake Mills farm in Buckinghamshire. Another popular visit was to Bibbies farm near Birkenhead on the Wirral. Such trips were well supported in the 1950s. *Ivy Evans, Berriew*

Mid-Wales Motorways acquired the space between St Mary's Church and the fellmongers yard. A building that was an office that would now be listed was demolished. The depot moved to the horse repository in 1948 and the office was purchased in Severn Square. This old temperance hotel was renamed Transport House until sold again in the late 1980s. *Ivy Evans, Berriew*

The *Bedford Magazine* for February 1951 had a major feature on MWM. Ivy has retained a pristine condition copy and John used the original prints for a project. The prints may have been gratis copies to his father who was then company Secretary. There is a wealth of information in this picture. The Bedford OB has just descended The Fox's Pitch and is crossing the Mochdre brook. The terraced houses were built many years previously for a wool mill. The snow sludge on the road site would be deep snow further up the valley at the Pentre.

Ivy Evans, Berriew and John Griffiths, Aberhafesp

A paradise of the older Bedfords lined up outside the horse repository at Newtown. The 1931 14-seat WHB (EP 5095 ex-Evans, New Mills) was the then veteran of the fleet and is in the centre. The reconditioned £60 coach is on the extra right. Various versions of 12 cwt Bedford vans were occasionally converted to buses with 7 seats. The position of the spare wheel would indicate the BYC series (EP 6546 ex-Tudors of Welshpool) in production from 1934 to 1937. The vehicle just behind was the fleet service van and Bill Cross describes driving this van following the mass Sunday school trip in 1948. *Bedford Magazine*

to the new company. The large office called Transport House in Severn Street was sold and a smaller office was rented. Soon Ivy's duties became part time and she finally retired in 1996 after 50 years' continuous service.

The bus company was well managed. The increasing number of cars caused a decline in passenger numbers with fare increases to create the situation where most fare stages were not viable. The only daily service to Adfa and New Mills in 2004 is the Post Office minibus. In 1946, the bus on Monday (Welshpool market) and Tuesday (Newtown market) would be crowded not only with local people but much of their produce. The gangway became a combination of standing passengers, eggs, butter and dressed poultry. Collecting fares was not easy. The bus had a roof rack with access via a rear ladder and would be laden with rabbits, ducks, cases and prams. Once the bus had started when a lady exclaimed 'Where is my baby?' The bus stopped, the driver collected the baby from the pram on the roof rack and the journey continued! The Newtown fair day was the last Tuesday in every month. Up to six MWM buses left the Gravel Park at 5.30 pm to many parts of the county. The company ticket inspector A.W. Hunt would be checking for any fare dodgers. He was a retired policeman with stern authority.

The late 1940s saw up to five services on a Saturday from Adfa to Newtown. The first left Adfa at 9.00 am and returned from Newtown at 12.30. An afternoon bus left Adfa at 1.15 pm and returned from Newtown at 4.00 pm. It immediately returned from Adfa to collect the remaining shoppers at 6.00 pm. There were two further services for both houses of the cinema leaving Newtown at 8.45 pm and 10.45 pm. The last bus could be a little rowdy and would have a strong smell of beer before the Welsh Sabbath settled on the villages. One lad should have been on the Carpenters bus to Bishops Castle and not arriving in Adfa around 11.30 pm.

Bedford WTB VJ 9128 is on the Montgomery service and is grinding up the long and steep incline of the Vastre between Newtown and Kerry. Note the extra accomodation fitted to the roof for the carriage of goods. *The Bedford Magazine*

A Bedford Duple is parked for a photograph on the Mochdre brook bridge. The bridge would be, and remains, typical of narrow bridges often with weight restriction over the fast flowing streams coming down from the uplands into the Severn valley. The land either side of the bridge is farmed by Coleg Powys and the author, Brian Poole, would often have taken tractors, cattle and sheep over this bridge until he retired. *The Bedford Magazine*

A group of Bedfords at the Gravel Park in Newtown on a cold wet Tuesday fair day during the winter of 1950/51. Most would be MWM coaches but some thought that the Owens family from Berriew owned one coach. Up to six MWM coaches left to Staylittle, Llandyssil, Brooks, New Mills, Mochdre, Bwlch-y-ffridd, etc. as well as Ithon Valley to Llanbadarn, Owens to Knighton, Carpenters to Bishops Castle and Owens of Berriew to Pant-y-ffridd. Uncle Ned is the man with the flat cap and raincoat in the right foreground. *The Bedford Magazine*

The New Mills bus leaves Newtown to travel via Aberbechan, Bettws and Treygynon. The bus park can be seen in the background. This is now a car park opposite the Post Office. This sector of road is now one way with traffic lights for vehicles and pedestrians. There is a designated bus route to the railway station close to this point from the current Back Lane bus station. *The Bedford Magazine*

Bodywork repair was carried out at the horse repository depot. Some of the lathes, sewing machines and hoists were still in the corner of this depot in 2005. Jack Worthington ex-Rolls Royce is on the left, Alec Willets is in the centre and Bill Sable is the panel beater on the right. UN 7783 was purchased from Davies of Leighton near Welshpool. *The Bedford Magazine*

Most independent companies purchased second-hand coaches. The fitters developed a range of skills to keep older buses in operating conditions. This is the interior of a 1936 Bedford WTB that was given a full internal renovation. In 1950, this vehicle was 14 years of age and many local independents will renovate a vehicle of 15 years-plus to continue to get a further few years of service. There is nothing new in the art of keeping older vehicles in service. *The Bedford Magazine*

Ivy recalls the huge Sunday school outing for the Newtown churches and chapels in 1947 and 1948. Such activities stopped during World War II and any beach suitable for landing was covered with defence steel and wire. Once these were cleared, the beach resorts of the Cambrian coast boomed for both rail and the coach companies. The bus company had to honour all the stage routes for the day of the outing but had no school buses working. All the company coaches were in use and Ivy can recall the orders and the invoices from others that were hired in for the day.

A national one-day strike took place in October 1955. The four Directors drove the school buses and the two main carriage routes of Newtown/ Welshpool/Shrewsbury and Newtown/Kerry/ Montgomery/Churchstoke/ Welshpool were driven by non-union labour. In retrospect, the strike was an error for it hastened car ownership and sharing a private car.

The offices were flooded in 1960 when the Severn was in full spate. All the old record books and other artefacts were soaked and all had to be destroyed. It was a heart breaking mess. Sadly a fire caused much damage in the yard in July 1967. Ten buses were destroyed including one that was only three weeks old. Two further buses were then written off and the insurance claim totalled £30,000. Within a few days, replacement buses had come in and other companies can be extremely generous with help. The Shrewsbury service had turned from profit to a loss and somewhere around 1969, the licence was surrendered to the traffic commissioners and Crosville took on that service.

Buses continued in use long after such models had ceased to be used in urban areas. Some of these buses were finally scrapped but vintage enthusiasts purchased some. Bedford EP 9982 was taken to Barry Docks and sailed for the West Indies. MFM 39 was hired to a film company for over a month to make a film called *Bus to Bosworth* (*see Chapter Ten*)

The bus company played a vital cultural and economic role within the county. Ivy has travelled thousands of miles on public transport. It was and should remain a way of meeting many interesting people and making friends.

Retrenchment, survival and new concepts

John Griffiths returned from London in 1979 to become the main shareholder and Managing Director of MWM. His father, the late T. Sidney Griffiths joined the company as Secretary in 1945 and was closely connected with its varying fortunes over the post-war years. Sidney became a Director and Chairman when the new company was formed in 1963.

John had contracted polio in 1950. The legacy has been a problem with full mobility. John completed his 'highers' and took on work in engineering at Cardiff with Guest, Keen & Nettlefolds. The Newtown to Cardiff express would come down with his clean laundry and take his used laundry back to mum in Newtown with *no* parcel charge. He could also come home for a weekend gratis on one of Dad's coaches.

John has retained his project submitted for his Higher School Certificate based on the Mid-Wales company. It contains maps of all the stage routes and

MID-WALES MOTORWAYS, Ltd

OLD CHURCH PLACE, NEWTOWN 'Phone 345

With the return of peace we are now able to supply transport for Private Parties, up-to-date Coaches, and we solicit your patronage and enquiries.

Don't forget that all passengers travelling by road are insured with unlimited indemnity.

'Phone 345  **'Phone 345**

MID-WALES MOTORWAYS, Ltd

TRANSPORT HOUSE,
SEVERN SQUARE, NEWTOWN

We specialise in catering for Private Parties up to any distance wit up-to-date Coaches, and we solicit your patronage and enquiries.

WE ALSO SPECIALISE IN CATERING FOR SUNDAY SCHOOL ANNUAL OUTINGS.

Don't forget that all passengers travelling by road are insured with unlimited indemnity.

Top: Services can now resume for private use, 1945.
The Cedewain Magazine

Above: The administration is now from Transport House, Severn Square, 1949.
The Cedewain Magazine

Sidney (*right*) retires and succession moves to John (*far right*), his son, who has opted to return after many years in London.
John Griffiths, Aberhafesp and The County Times

passenger statistics. The firm was the largest private bus company in Mid-Wales. It had a total of over 60 buses and all were single-deckers. Around 100 staff was employed in driving, conducting, repair and administration. The main depot was at Newtown and there were sub-depots at convenient points to cover the rural nature of the surrounding countryside. Examples from some of John's tables now follow:

Stage passengers 1951 to 1952
July 93,298; August 97,662; September 89,195; October 100,615; November 90,393; December 82,143; January 87,201; March 79,468; April 85,906; May 82,067; June 83,447; Total 1,037,770: mean 86,481. The reduction caused by more petrol availability and increasing number of vans and cars can already be discerned.

Passengers carried	*June to Aug 1951*	%	*Sept to Nov 1951*	%
Stage	277,031	79.5	261,176	76.7
Express	3,114	0.9	1,375	0.4
Excursion	6,008	1.7	1,082	0.3
Private hire	16,142	4.7	6,454	1.9
Schools	45,968	13.2	70,304	20.7
Total	348,353		340,391	

Most companies would find that the percentage between schools and stage would be reversed within 20 years. Note the way the company can dovetail extra excursions and private hire with school reduction in summer holidays.

The Newtown to Cardiff express operated daily from Easter to September and every other day for the remainder of the year. An investigation took place on a North Wales service operating from Newtown via Welshpool, Llanfyllin, Bala, Ffestiniog, Llandudno to Bangor but it never came about.

British Railways still had all stations open between Shrewsbury and Aberystwyth , Llanidloes and Whitchurch and the branch line to Llanfyllin. The BTC usually gave the replacement bus services to Crosville when closure occurred and the independents struggled. The only one operating was the Welshpool to Shrewsbury intermediate stations service that was granted by the traffic commissioners before closure of rural stations such as Westbury and Yockleton.

Both John and several other people have retained copies of articles written about the company. The *Bedford Magazine* of February 1951 had a Mochdre bus on the front cover. R.H. Carse wrote the article. Bedfords accounted for 36 of the now total fleet of 65 buses and coaches with a policy of light Bedford OBs for the village duties and the heavy 'oilers' for the larger capacity inter-town routes. There were 49 stage routes operating over 830 miles. The service carried medical and veterinary supplies as well as the expected daily papers and magazines plus shop and workshop sundries. An unusual feature was that of an after hours service licence so that services could be completed because of inclement weather. We have included several photographic prints from this article.

Another article is that published by the *Commercial Motor* in September 1959, written by G. Duncan Jewell. The optimism of 1951 had evaporated as the financial situation started to deteriorate from 1953 onwards. The company had acquired the Welshpool to Shrewsbury direct route despite railway opposition. The route

Right: Example of tours available in 1982.
John Griffiths, Aberhafesb

Below: Notepad heading for detailing enquiries *circa* 1982 showing three Bedford coaches in the Newtown Back Lane Park.
John Griffiths, Aberhafesb

MID-WALES MOTORWAYS LTD.

BACK LANE, NEWTOWN, POWYS, SY16 2PW
Telephone: NEWTOWN 26345

Continental Holidays 1982

April 3rd Lloret de Mar, Spain .... 14 days £178 F.B.
April 9th Paris, mini-break .... 3 days £43 B&B
● April 16th Amsterdam — Floriade '82 .... 4 days £56 B&B
● May 14th Rimini — Italian tour .... 10 days £150 F.B.
May 28th Paris & Versailles .... 4 days £56 B&B
June 4th Brussels & Bruges .... 4 days £56 B&B
● June 24th Blanes, Costa Brava .... 11 days £175 H.B.
● July 16th Switzerland — Interlaken ..... 10 days £185 H.B.
July 23rd Paris .... 10 days £154 B&B
July 23rd Burgundy .... 10 days £164 H.B.
● Aug. 6th Brittany .... 10 days £154 H.B.
Aug. 13th Paris .... 10 days £154 B&B
Aug. 20th Normandy & Loire Valley ...... 9 days £165 H.B.
● Aug. 27th Austria — Innsbruck .... 10 days £180 H.B.
● Sept. 8th Rhine Valley Tour .... 10 days £170 H.B.
Oct. 1st Wieze Beer Festival .... 3 days £49 B&B

● *Courier Service on the New Bova Continental*

To avoid disappointment phone or write for further details soon.
No feeders! We pick you up on the way through in Mid-Wales, Shrewsbury, Telford.

MID-WALES MOTORWAYS LTD.

TRANSPORT HOUSE, SEVERN SQUARE, NEWTOWN

Telephone: NEWTOWN 26345

Passenger Transport Operators of Public Services
TOURS and PRIVATE PARTY HIRE Coaches

A fleet of 29 to 53 seater modern coaches are at your service and your enquiries are invited.

We are LICENSED to operate Day Tours to all parts of Great Britain, and also operate extended eight and four day private party Continental Tours, from both the Newtown and Welshpool Areas.

Enquiries to:
TRANSPORT HOUSE, NEWTOWN (Phone 26345); and POWYS TRAVEL SERVICES, HIGH STREET, WELSHPOOL (Phone 2966).

expanded and warranted a double-decker service for a few years. In 1952 total passenger numbers (stage/express) were 1,245,134 but by 1958 the total was only 77 per cent at 961,840. Wages and fuel had increased, higher fares could not cover the widening gap and the main saving grace was the rapid increase in one-man operation. Heavy diesels were still not considered for the total fleet because many of the secondary routes were on poor foundation roads. The large increase in privately-owned cars within the rural community had caused 14 out of 35 services to be withdrawn and the vehicle fleet reduced from 58 to 47 vehicles.

The final article is entitled 'Border Line History' by A. Moyes in *Buses Extra*, October 1977. The problem of one of the largest independents shows that rural traffic potential is not sufficient to build a strong and consistently prosperous company and that the early post-war euphoria would be shattered. Post-Suez fuel costs caused many rural operators to retrench and several enquiries followed.

The Jacks Committee (November 1959) started to consider some form of support but had no outcome. The Llanfair depot closed in August 1963 and then the company ceased to trade in the following month. It was reformed as Mid-Wales Motorways 1963. The new slimmer company set out to retain the business centred on Newtown/Welshpool with a concentration on school contracts and excursion private hire. Crosville took on the Cardiff express and the direct Shrewsbury route also went to Crosville after the Newtown fire. Soon the green Crosville Bristol bus became common with an outstation in Welshpool cattle market. A rural fuel rebate became available but involved much form filling. John recalls that the précis from these three articles covers the history between 1945 and 1979 when his father was company Secretary. He can almost read his father's style answering these three men.

The company had already started UK and Continental Tours when John took over in 1979. John never took a PSV test because of his polio but he was soon travelling by car to arrange the hotels, the routes and the ferry crossings. The Rimini and the Venice trip became very popular. The company started to use the then new Plymouth to Santander ferry for a route to the Costa Brava. Development was under way for a market in Croatia and Slovenia but political problems were already on the horizon.

Bus deregulation followed in October 1986 and this included abolition of route licensing. John regrets that the company had not been nationalized in the late 1940s as compensation may have earned more with fewer headaches in another industry. The company was then one of the largest independents not brought into state ownership. The company only had the Newtown urban route and a handful of market day stage routes by 1979. The 1986 Act would have finished rural stage services. The political problem was soon apparent and this led to a new system of tendering for subsidized services with the County Councils.

John persuaded Harold Beadles to merge his company in 1979. This would make better use of resources especially that of school contract bidding. John was Chairman when the 50th anniversary was celebrated in 1987. Special trips and holidays were organized. The highlight was a May dinner in Newtown with guests and families from the early years joining the then present staff. John passed the company on to Selwyn Evans of Aberystwyth in August 1988 to

Re-issue 5.5.65

To be carried in, but not attached to, the Statutory Driving Licence

BRITISH RAILWAYS B.R. 14114

L.M. REGION

MOTOR DRIVER'S DOMESTIC LICENCE

Name (in full) E. W. FRANCIS

Station WELSHPOOL Dept. GOODS

Groups of Vehicles authorised to drive	Examiner's Signature	Date
Group 1. Rigid vehicles up to and including 3 tons capacity	A.B. Watkins	8.4.63
Group 2. Articulated vehicles up to and including 3 tons capacity	A.B. Watkins	17.5.63
Group 3. Rigid vehicles exceeding 3 tons capacity ...	J.H. Holloway	5.12.66
Group 4. Articulated vehicles exceeding 3 tons capacity TWO SPEED AXLE	J.H. Holloway	5.12.66
~~Group 5.~~ Tractors including articulated tractive units when used for hauling drawbar trailers...		
Group 6. Road Motor Horse Boxes		
Group 7 DIESEL ENGINED VEHICLES	A.B. Watkins	8.4.63

The holder of this licence is not authorised to drive any type of British Railways Board vehicle other than stated above and is not authorised to drive on the highway unless he holds a Statutory driving licence.

VEHICLES FITTED WITH ... TWO SPEED AXLES

Above: Eddie started his driving career with British Railways (BR). It was necessary to have an internal (BR) licence. Eddie's licence shows his career progress with the examiner coming down from Crewe to endorse his skill.

Eddie Francis and Mid-Wales Motorways

Right: Eddie with Bedford TK tractor now trading as National Carriers at Barmouth around 1973 on the daily circular route of Newtown, Machynlleth, Barmouth, Trawsfynydd, Bala, Corwen, Llangollen, Ruabon and Shrewsbury to change trailers at Shrewsbury and park overnight in the Newtown goods yard. This route follows many closed railway lines of the 1960s.

Eddie Francis and Mid-Wales Motorways

concentrate on other interests. Harold opted to take his share out and recommence his own bus company. The head office is no longer at Newtown but maintains a booking office and a main depot there. John Griffiths now qualifies for a free bus pass. Eddie Francis brings the story up to date in the following section.

The new name of Mid Wales Travel

The Newtown transport manager for the company was Eddie Francis. Mid-Wales Motorways 1963 remains a registered name even though Mid Wales Travel is written on the vehicles. The company head office and ownership is now with Evans of Penrhyncoch at Aberystwyth. Maybe the name had to change for the word 'motorway' has a very different meaning from that of 1937.

Eddie's transport career started with British Railways as relief lorry driver at Newtown. Nine lorries operated from the station in 1961. Eddie had to have an additional operating licence from British Railways and an examiner from Crewe endorsed this. He was upgraded from a rigid van under 3 tons to articulated vehicles and diesel engine operation.

Change was constant in the 1960s as the industry altered. He was to operate the replacement to the early mail train after the Mid-Wales line had closed. He would report for duty at 4.30 am and would load with papers, mail, milk and fresh fish by 5.15 am. Deliveries would be made at Llandinam, Llanidloes, Tylwch, Pant-y-dŵr, St Harmon, Rhayader, Builth Road, Builth and Llandrindod. He would then return on the same route collecting parcels to arrive back around 1.30 pm. Llanidloes station still had facilities for parcels until the line closed for freight in May 1964. (The line re-opened for Clywedog cement trains until 1967.) Eddie would take a lorry with parcels to Llanidloes and then he would deliver feeds and fertiliser from covered wagons to the farms. The parcel lorry ceased at Llanidloes in May 1964 and another duty after this date would be to take the Scammel three-wheel tug with trailer from Newtown and then deliver round the Llanidloes area. Newtown non-bulk goods ceased in 1967, rail delivery was to Welshpool and goods for Newtown were collected by road. Then Welshpool closed and the rail depot became Shrewsbury and even Stoke for certain goods. Eddie would follow the routes of closed lines by the early 1970s. The goods transport section of British Railways became the National Freight Corporation with 'National Carriers' painted on the lorry with yellow livery. One of the final routes was to start at Newtown (fully loaded the previous evening at Shrewsbury) and head over to Machynlleth, then to Barmouth, back to Dolgellau, then to Trawsfynydd, over the mountains to Bala, then Corwen and Llangollen and head back to Shrewsbury to hitch to an already loaded trailer to park overnight at Newtown again.

One of the Welshpool men had a PSV licence and earned some extra money with weekend coach/bus driving. Eddie decided to try for the same goal and took the test in a borrowed Mid-Wales Motorways bus. He was to work a minibus for Geoff Williams of Kerry as well as some driving for MWM. The rail-

Right: Roy Poston converted the Bedford TK ex-Woodhouse (local haulage contractor) artic tractor into the breakdown and recovery unit. The bus behind is a Bedford Duple so the photograph must date from the 1980s. Roy Poston used the same crane to convert the current vehicle on site in 2005. It is a Ford artic tractor with a V8 Deutz diesel and has enough power to recover most vehicles.

Eddie Francis and Mid-Wales Motorways

Below: GAL 19J was an unusual Bedford Willowbrook bus parked in the Newtown yard in 1986. It is still in red from the previous bus company and it was the ex-Laura Ashley works bus. The reduction of a manufacturing base in Britain during the 1990s would have led to the withdrawal of many works buses across shifts. This Willowbrook was thought to be on the shorter YRQ chassis with the engine moved to mid-chassis. A Willowbrook bus was not common either within the National Bus Company (with about 50 ordered by United Counties), or the independents.

Graham Sharp

Eddie Francis stands by the Bedford Duple while part-time driver Malcolm Price stands by a non PSV (less than 8 ton) Ford. The Ford was a local feeder from Cefn-y-coed area to Abermule Primary School. The Bedford was used to bring older pupils to Newtown High School.

Eddie Francis and Mid-Wales Motorways

The bus arrival/departure point at Llanfair Caereinion. There are two Leylands from MWM waiting to take secondary school children back to Newtown. The school has a major stream for Welsh First Language for a larger catchment area than the Llanfair area.

Eddie Francis and Mid-Wales Motorways

The Newtown line up around 1990 shows a complete line of Bedfords. From left to right are Duple, Laser, Plaxton, Duple, Plaxton and Duple. *Eddie Francis and Mid-Wales Motorways*

F211 FAW came on site as a new vehicle on lease hire. It was a full executive vehicle with toilet, video and beverage machine. It was used on tours and also for a long distance feeder into London for continental stage route express connections. It was working the Fishguard Irish ferry connection to London when it overturned on black ice near Llanelli. No one was hurt but the bus was an insurance write off. Roy Poston recollects collecting the vehicle from a Carmarthen yard. *Eddie Francis and Mid-Wales Motorways*

The Leyland coach was purchased from Robinsons, one of the big tour operators and re-sprayed from the original green to Mid Wales Travel white. The coach is parked in hotel grounds near Dumfries in Galloway. *Eddie Francis and Mid-Wales Motorways*

The last Bedford owned by MWM is seen in Welshpool High Street on the stage route to Montgomery. This Bedford Plaxton was finally sold on during the summer of 2002. *Eddie Francis and Mid-Wales Motorways*

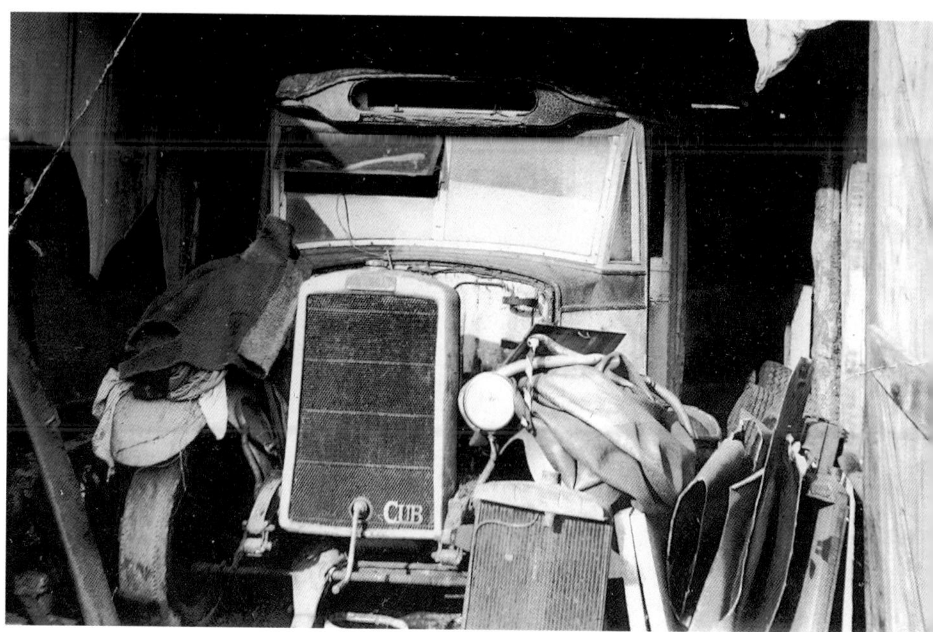

The Williams Leyland Tiger Cub KP3 (*circa* 1934) was scrapped by MWM in 1953 and became a chicken shed in the Hundred of Hendidley to the west of Newtown. Harold arranged to purchase it as seen at the farm with a view to restoration. The bus was taken to Beadles bus yard and placed under cover. The original aluminium radiator block has been replaced from a later Cub model. The bus was still in the yard in 2005. This bus would travel from Halfway House via Rowton, Alberbury, Crew Green, Llandrinio, Crab Tree Turn, Four Crosses, Llanymynech, Pant, Llynclys and on to Oswestry in 1945. In 1925, passengers could have boarded the Ford railcar on the Criggion branch at Criggion or Llandrinio Road or Crew Green for connections at Kinnerley to either Shrewsbury or Llanymynech. *Harold Beadles, Newtown*

Two Shropshire companies, Williams of Halfway House and Bunces of Worthen joined MWM around 1939. Bunces' bus, UX 7358, struggles in deep snow at Rowley on the Shropshire side of the Long Mountain. All snow had to be shovelled by hand in the mid-1930s. The make of the coach is uncertain but Bunces brought Tilling Stevens into the fleet.

John Green, Bishops Castle

related services finished in 1981; redundancy and severance pay followed. MWM offered a contract of six months for the summer only. Eddie without a passport had never even left the UK and suddenly found himself in Austria, Spain, Italy etc. British Railways offered Eddie work on the permanent way (trackside duties) the following winter so he worked from a crew lorry on such duties as shovelling ballast. MWM offered a full time contract in 1987. The company soon changed hands and the older Director-drivers retired. Eddie found himself in charge of the Newtown depot in 1991. The depot works school contracts, factory works buses, stage routes, day trips and tours. The fleet of around 20 buses, mainly Bedfords, of the mid-1980s had contracted to the fleet at December 2004 of an executive Leyland Plaxton, and ex-Midland Red Leyland 53-seater, a Leyland Tiger, plus two Mercedes Midi buses and several minibuses. The Newtown fleet has stabilized around this number for a decade. Extra buses and drivers are drawn from the pool between Aberystwyth and Newtown as required. The buses can work a hard long day dovetailing with factory, then school, plus stage routes and evening duties as required. The last Bedford was KEW 964T and the long illustrious partnership of MWM and Bedford came to a conclusion in the summer of 2002.

A Shropshire connection recalls Williams of Halfway House

The Halfway House is a community between Welshpool and Shrewsbury. It is the first village on the A458 on the Shropshire Plain. A view to the west looks into the uplands of the Welsh border. John Green, now of Bishops Castle, recalls his grandfather, Ernest Williams, and the family bus company. The Williams joined MWM prior to World War II. Ernest may well have started elements of trading in the motor industry before 1914 when he would deliver five gallons of petrol (Pratts) to the few 'toffs' that had automobiles. Two petrol stations and garages expanded from this humble beginning. The first commercial vehicle would almost certainly have been an ex-War Department lorry soon after 1919. This would have had multiple-use and soon had benches to take locals to Welshpool and Oswestry markets. Several purpose-built buses would have followed from about 1925 onwards.

John Green was born in 1932 and spent much time with his grandparents. John would only have a child's memory of the pre-amalgamation period but is certain that there were two buses and the pride and joy of the fleet was the Leyland Tiger Cub. Grandfather became Director of MWM and took his turn as Chairman. The depot at Halfway House continued for many years both during and after the war. John would often be with his grandfather and started to help. The conductress was Aunt Joan and the driver would be grandad, Uncle Reg or Uncle Dennis. There was a wartime route from Trewern to Shrewsbury granted by the Traffic Commission to move workers to key factories. There was only a tenuous bus connection to Welshpool and Newtown but Buttington station and junction was only a mile further on from Trewern. The other stage routes to Welshpool and Oswestry on respective market days squeezed through every narrow lane to small hamlets. People just pushed on until the bus was packed

Right: Thomas Green, son in law of Ernest Williams of Halfway House worked for MWM after World War II. He purchased the Worthen Motors section to set up his own business of Worthen Motorways in 1963. KUP 949 is an ex-Southdown Leyland (head office at Brighton). It is parked outside Montgomery Town Hall in the 1970s as a vintage vehicle.
John Green, Bishops Castle

Dad certainly purchased some MWM buses when he went independent. John has several MWM photographs but they may not necessarily be units that Greens would own. The indicator board indicates Montgomery via Sarn. This picture is one of several coaches that had a Perkins engine (see circles emblem on radiator) fitted during the Suez fuel crisis to increase fuel economy. Excess vibration then became a problem. *John Green, Bishops Castle*

and any regulation on numbers standing was ignored. John would often help during school holidays and his duty was to climb up the rear ladder to place prams and bulky crates on the roof rack. People sat on their seats with a tower of eggs, rabbits and vegetables on their laps and these goods would disappear quickly during the period of wartime rationing. The interior would totally disappear in humid steam on days of heavy rain.

The depot had buses allocated including the Leyland Tiger Cub but sometimes another bus was transferred from Newtown because of major repairs or company requirements. The Bedford was truly the ideal country bus. Civilian workers' transport was required to support developments at Criggion and at the War Department depots centred at Kinnerley. The company and the depot were both profitable during the war. One of the clearest memories John had was the cold morning frost in the wartime yard. The sump oil was thick and all the petrol-engined buses had to be started on the handle. Several drivers would swing the engine for successful ignition and then keep the engine speed up for several minutes. The shed would fill with blue smoke and noise.

Tom Green, John's father, served with the military and returned on demobilization. Worthen Motors would be the final company to join MWM bringing in the direct Montgomery to Shrewsbury route. Tom was the manager for Worthen Motors and his office moved to Newtown after the merger as his role extended to the total company. Dad purchased the Worthen section in 1963 taking on the stage routes and school contracts. The company was to trade as Worthen Motorways. The business was sold on earlier than expected due to Tom's ill health. It was finally sold to David Pye, one of the staff. John worked in other sectors and finally became the Registrar of births, deaths, civil-weddings etc. for West Shropshire until retirement. John would help his father at weekends including when the company was part of MWM. He had a PSV licence both for driving and conducting and visited most seaside resorts in Wales from Porthcawl in the South to Pwllheli in the North-West as well as the Lancashire coast resorts such as Southport and Blackpool.

The single-deck Bedfords had a sliding manually-operated door rather than the open entrance at the rear as for most half-cab buses whether a single- or a double-decker. The police once stopped this bus on the outskirts of Shrewsbury to check that the door dispensation operator (the conductor) was at the correct part of the bus when the vehicle stopped or drew away from a stage route. John cannot remember the full timetable but there was an early bus for workers and the return around 5.30 pm from Shrewsbury. There was a regular clientele so the bus would sound the horn if one of the passengers were missing. Suddenly some one would rush down a path still with traces of shaving soap or the remnants of marmalade and toast! There were extra buses on Saturdays for shoppers and this would also include a 10.30 pm departure for cinemagoers. There were several Sunday services also.

The problem of the early return from Shrewsbury (8.30 am) was that it would be empty and the same occurred when a bus left Montgomery around 4.00 pm to collect the workers on the their return journey. No one has ever solved the problem of commuter flows. The stage route loading change between 1950 and 1960 was immense. No one could blame the customers for their dream of

MWM owned several Commers. CEP 599 is at the Shrewsbury bus station awaiting departure to Montgomery in the 1950s. This area is now a short-term car park and the wood-framed building is now part of the Rowley Museum and Art Gallery. Several of these Commers were still on the stock list of 1975 and are listed as Bedfords. The reason was that the Commer petrol engines were replaced by Bedford diesels. This Commer is one of several that were purchased from Glyn Bayley of Newtown. *John Green, Bishops Castle*

Tom Green stands by a Ford coach in the yard at Worthen. David Pye, Tom's successor, would move the depot to the redundant Minsterley railway station in the early 1970s.
John Green, Bishops Castle

acquiring a private car, as rural services were sparse. The ratio of business was rapidly altering and the valued Local Education Authority (LEA) school contracts in both Montgomeryshire and Shropshire must have kept many companies afloat. The succession to David Pye and his company of Worthen Motors can be found in the Welshpool section in Chapter Eight.

Mid-Wales Motorways and the Sentinels

The company was not only the owner of four Sentinel buses but also continued to use them for up to 19 years. The Sentinel factory was in Shrewsbury. It was almost certain that their sales staff would have worked hard to secure an order from MWM. The buses were deployed on the direct route from Newtown/Welshpool to Shrewsbury and the quieter route via Montgomery as well as other duties. The four buses are still remembered by several drivers, long retired fitters and passengers. The passage of time has caused memories to be that of considerable affection.

Sentinel was noted for locomotives and steam lorries. A Sentinel Dorman operated on the internal railway for the construction of the Clywedog dam at Llanidloes and a Sentinel steam locomotive operated at the Criggion quarries near Welshpool on the Shropshire and Montgomeryshire light railway branch until around 1950. Sentinel started to diversify into diesel power for road transport prior to World War II. They also acquired ownership and the design of the Gilford bus and coach company. A licence was obtained to produce a Ricardo indirect injection diesel engine. The engine was quiet, smooth running and had adequate power. However, it was also complex, consumed excess fuel and had a tendency to overheat. The under-floor mounting was suspect and the whole unit could fail.

The DV4 lorry (diesel vehicle with four cylinders) fitted with the Sentinel Ricardo horizontal engine went on general sale in 1947. Production exceeded 1,000 units plus over a period of eight years. The 14 ft 9 in. wheelbase version was selected as the basis of a new bus. The first units used Beadles coachwork. Later, many were fully constructed in-house.

The Sentinel was the first bus on the open market with an engine under the floorboards between the axles with front entrance ahead of the front axle. It had a capacity of 40 seats compared with 35 for half-cabs and created much interest. Ribble of Preston, one of the large provincials, placed an order for 14 units. A further order for six with six cylinders for the Lake District hill routes followed. No further orders were received from any of the BET companies. Sales were not good. There were few exports so the sole customers were the independents. Several other coachbuilders produced both Sentinel buses and coaches.

The engine was now plagued with difficulty. Sentinel took a gamble to establish confidence: they offered to fit the engine by altering the block to take direct injection equipment. This would be free of charge to all with a warranty. Sadly, the perceived and real problems were now deeply entrenched and sales were below that of financial viability. All four MWM Sentinels were STC 4/40s with Sentinel bodies and three had the altered Ricardo engines. The total production was only 147 units between 1948 and 1957. The pioneer design set a

The Shingler family has lived on the borders in the Welshpool area for several generations. The steamer (thought to be a Clayton) was one of five operated by Wilf's grandfather. The young lad in the centre is Bill Shingler, Wilf's father. *Wilf Shingler, Halfway House, Shropshire*

Below left: Bill Shingler, with PSV disc, was one of the Mid-Wales drivers in the 1950s working from the Welshpool depot. The Crossley coach is about to depart on a Saturday excursion to the seaside at Barmouth. *Wilf Shingler, Halfway House, Shropshire*

Below right: The Shrewsbury firm, Sentinel, produced the last steam lorry for export in 1949. The company started to fabricate a forward control 7/8 ton lorry with the Ricardo under-floor diesel engine in 1947. An early model was sold to the local firm of W.J.F. so the factory could monitor and eliminate any design fault. Bill Shingler was the driver keeping the detailed record. The DV4 with the 14 ft 9 in. wheelbase was to become the chassis for the Sentinel bus. The first few buses had a radiator similar to this lorry. *Wilf Shingler, Halfway House, Shropshire*

This is the under-floor Ricardo diesel fitted to the Sentinel STC4 bus. TC may stand for town and country. This is a posed picture in the area of Whitchurch Road near the Sentinel factory. Wilf Shingler cannot say with full certainty that the driver was his father. Certainly Bill took his turn on the Shrewsbury-Welshpool stage route and continued to hone his considerable knowledge of driving Sentinels. *Mid Wales Travel Site Office, Newtown*

CEP 147 was delivered new to MWM in May 1951 and remained with the company until the ill-fated fire. Note the entry light and steps all within good view of the driver. The bus is parked in the Newtown depot. *Ann Evans, Newtown*

GUX 524 parked at the Newtown depot. The advert for the *Wellington Journal & Shrewsbury News* represents additional income for the company and reflects the fact that these Sentinels usually worked into Shrewsbury with far greater buying power than Newtown or Welshpool. Every day these buses almost travelled back to the factory that fabricated them in the early 1950s.

Ann Evans, Newtown

A. Moyes took this photograph in June 1969 one month before the yard fire that destroyed three of the four Sentinels. The buses are parked in the Newtown yard. OUA 76 was a Commer with an unusual Saunders Roe body. The first owner is thought to have been an airport authority and it may have been at Gatwick when that airport was new. Many would have the opinion that the design of the Sentinel body was aesthetically attractive and functional while the Commer looks bulbous and clumsy.

David Hughes Collection

The beginning. BEP 864 has just been delivered, brand new, from the Sentinel works for the first of many journeys between Newtown and Shrewsbury. The vehicle displays 'Shrewsbury, Mid-Wales, Cardiff'; the company was very proud of the Cardiff Express route but it was a very small fraction of turnover for them. Retired staff doubt if the Sentinel ever went to Cardiff.

Harold Beadles, Newtown

The conclusion. Arthur Rowe and Giovanni Colucci look at the destruction caused by the fire in July 1967 in the Newtown yard. Giovanni would have travelled by Mid-Wales Motorways in 1944 as a POW to various farms. The rear of the undamaged GUX 524 can be seen in the top left-hand corner. The fire almost certainly prevented one of the Sentinels being transferred for preservation as some of the independents became a Mecca for the restoration of vintage buses. The Newtown to Shrewsbury licence for operation would transfer to Crosville later as the firm struggled to recover.

Harold Beadles, Newtown

The placing of the Ricardo diesel engine under-floor would have been logical to a Sentinel engineer. The steam engine is seen placed in the same position on an earlier Sentinel lorry. A good glow in the firebox would pass the necessary steam to the engine. The vehicle is seen at Llanfair Caereinion Railway station. *Author*

Two destroyed Sentinels including BEP 864 caused by the wrong glow. The heat ruptured the main derv tank sending diesel across the yard so the fire spread quickly. The police and forensic experts came to no conclusion. The fire started within the site office and may have been arson or a fault. *Don Griffiths, Newtown (The County Times)*

After the fire all that was left of 13 coaches was a twisted tangle of metal.

standard. Both Leyland and AEC followed with underfloor engines and achieved sales volumes with the BET companies and municipals. Midland Red had already established the principle for their internal supply.

The Sentinel bus was not an economic success but it set a standard that others followed. It is therefore significant within bus history. It would be typical of an independent such as MWM to persevere with such a pioneer design until the four units gave reasonable service for a long working life. It was ideal from about 1955 as legislation started to alter for one-man-operation to assist survival on rural routes.

A Miscellany of traces of the company

Many villages had a bus service in the 1920s and 1930s operated by one man/one bus. Most were amalgamated into a larger business and many pioneer services would be within MWM stage routes by the outbreak of World War II. These enterprises are now on the fringe of some older people's memories. An attempt has been made to trace several.

Richard Pryce of the Revel, Berriew was brought up in the village of Tregynon. His father started a transport business at Bwlch-y-ffridd in the partnership with his brother. The basic start was a lorry/bus that was used to carry livestock and was then cleaned out for passengers for the Tuesday and Saturday journey to Newtown. This was the only bus still used for livestock and passengers when Mid Wales took the bus into their yard in 1937.

'Dad' was not in the best of health, probably due to his experiences serving in World War I. Richard was only six when his father sold the bus and the route to MWM and he has no memory of the bus. His father continued with a lorry until around 1945 when he sold out to Jack Arthur of Kerry who then moved to live in the parish of Aberhafesb/ Bwlch-y-ffridd. Certainly Richard can remember that his father continued to hold a PSV licence and would help MWM during the war on a part time basis. One of the duties would be to distribute the evacuees around Newtown and the surrounding villages. They were collected from Newtown station and were children from Birkenhead. Richard came across several documents a few years ago when having a tidy-up. There was a bill of conveyance for the purchase of the bus. It was a very small sum reflecting that the lorry/bus had reached the end of a working life. Richard's cousin, Alun, continued in the lorry business and this continues today with a hay and straw business.

The older people of the parish can still recall the service when one of the characters was an old lady dressed in black and she had a very similar appearance to Granny in the Giles cartoons. One seat was kept for her only and she would berate anyone with her stick that tried to usurp her right. She acquired the affectionate nickname of 'Mad Mother Morgan'.

Cecil Bebb started a bus service from Kerry in the early 1920s. This direct route from village to town centre rapidly filched the passengers from the Kerry/Abermule branch railway. Cecil Bebb was a member of a large family and several younger members of the family still have traces of memory. Marie,

Right: The rear of the green Chevrolet can be seen behind Marie's mother. Cecil Bebb operated a frequent service from Kerry to Newtown and also up to the Anchor on the Kerry Ridgeway. Leslie Bebb is the only remaining member of that generation. He recalls that the bus body could be taken off and the Chevrolet could operate as a flat or have wooden railings added for cattle or sheep carriage.

Marie Hussey née Bebb, Kerry

Below: The Vulcan 6VF lorry may have been purchased from Pryce who had the Bwlch-y-ffridd Newtown bus service prior to 1937. The gantry for changing the lorry body between a flat and livestock stood in the yard at Aberhafesp for several decades. The system was and still is used for extending the hire use of livestock lorries. Jack Arthur, David's father, soon had a post-war Vulcan with metal cab, a Guy and a Bedford.

David Arthur, Newtown

his daughter, thinks that the bus stood as a derelict hulk in the corner of Kerry timber yard for a number of years. She thought that the owner of the timber yard requested permission to dispose of the hulk. It is likely that any paperwork or photographs were consumed in the bonfire. Marie has located a single photograph dated 1931 inherited from her mother. There is no way that Marie's mother would have ridden a motorcycle so the picture must have been staged. The young face in the rear of the Chevrolet is Marie's eldest brother. Marie would have been too young to have much recall of the service. It was thought that Neales purchased the Bebb bus and route in the mid-1930s.

No driver of the period during World War II can now be located. There are only a handful of men who can recall joining MWM after demobilization. Jim Cranwell was born in 1919. He served in the RAF as a regular joining well before the conflict commenced. He joined the bus company in 1945 after around 10 years in the RAF. He was one of the drivers for the mammoth convoy for the Sunday school trip of all the churches/chapels of Newtown to Aberystwyth in 1948.

He lived at Llandyssil and would cycle in to the Newtown depot. Much of his work before 1950 would have been on the two routes between Newtown and Welshpool. He was to work the Welshpool-Shrewsbury route once granted by the Traffic Commissioners around 1950. This started with a half-cab single-decker but was allocated to the Sentinels with the extra capacity. The route demand expanded rapidly and soon all 40 seats were taken with standing passengers in addition. More people started to work in shops, offices and factories in Shrewsbury from the villages between Welshpool and Ford. The company therefore purchased several Guy double-deckers to save putting on

Some of the MWM coaches in the park at Aberystwyth. The drivers from left to right are, *back row*: Jack Rees, Roy Owen, Ernie Evans; *front row*, Ifor Bennett and Des Meddins.

Harold Beadles, Newtown

Much effort has been made to secure a picture of the mass coach contract for the Sunday school trips. A phone call was received from Bob, the son of Jim. This is what Bob had located in a box not disturbed for decades in the attic. The fleet is lined up at the Aberystwyth coach park with each driver standing by his coach. The line includes Bedford WTBs and OBs with the half-cabs at the furthest point. The year could be 1947 but is more likely to be July 1948 when all the Sunday Schools of Newtown, churches and chapels, combined for the day. Ned Evans (Director) is the nearest and Jim is the second man in beside the Bedford WTB.

Jim Cranwell, Llandyssil

an extra bus. The drivers would always try to get the only one with the six-cylinder Gardner engine but John found the five-cylinder buses satisfactory provided the revs were kept up and skilful use was made of the gearbox. The noise of the counter-balanced five-cylinder Gardner must have been a distinctive rural bus sound just like the whine of the Bedford OB transmission.

The Sentinels were very good to drive because of the lower weight ratio to engine power. Such a vehicle as the Crossley half-cab had heavy steering but the diesel engine weight was on the front wheels. These would cut through any sheeting rain or ice on the then poorer road surface. Point the bus in the correct direction and that is where it would go. The Sentinels were light on steering and another skill was required as ice started to form on the road with a heavy frost. Buses left Welshpool around 6.30 am and 7.30 am for the workers and then ran back and forth until late evening. There were also several buses on a Sunday. The 50 hour week was therefore spread over a wide range of hours. Jim opted to transfer to the cycle factory in Newtown around 1955 for better hours.

One delightful duty was to drive the Daimler with the fluid flywheel and pre-selector on the newly established Newtown-Cardiff service. There was around a five-hour wait before the return so the driver would have a meal followed by a 'kip' on the back seat. (The interval between arrival and return of market day services must have given the opportunity for drivers to have a 'kip' in every part of the British Isles.) Jim would cover for the school contract Bedford OB so he would have almost certainly have taken the then young David Pye to secondary school from Llandyssil to Newtown.

Mr Neale one of the founders of Mid-Wales Motorways with school children. He had driven the school bus during a token strike. This picture was published in 15th October, 1955 edition of *Montgomeryshire Express* which also had an application from Mid-Wales Motorways to the North Western Traffic Authority to withdraw certain services as the company was trading at a loss and the reserve fund would soon be exhausted.

Harold retains some photographs of his time with Mid-Wales Motorways. This shows a typical Tuesday market day in the late 1940s at the Gravel at Newtown. A Guy half-cab is parked within a group of Bedfords. The Gravel can be a bitter place in winter. The buses were often parked for the day and the driver would be back well before departure so people could unload their purchases and sit down inside. *Harold Beadles Collection*

Bedford EP 9982 was purchased new on 24th March, 1948. It stands in the MWM yard at Newtown with three staff. Frank Bethel is on the coach, Bill Higley stands by the bodywork and Reg Meddins is by the door. Reg would become one of the Directors of Mid-Wales Motorways 1963. *Harold Beadles Collection*

Chapter Three

Other Independent Companies of Newtown

Harold Beadles and his company

Harold was brought up in Newtown. His family had no connection with the bus industry. Harold's first job, starting on 26th August, 1948, was with Mid-Wales Motorways at Old Church House as an apprentice fitter. Edward Evans was the Director responsible for the maintenance of vehicles. The initial duties were routine servicing and valeting. Engine and transmission overhaul such as clutch replacement was carried out as necessary. There were up 70 different buses/coaches to keep 'on the road' from the various depots. The company arranged for Harold to take his car test in 1950 so that he could take the van out. Next came National Service from 1953 to 1956 when there was an extension to 2½ years for a short period. Harold served with the Royal Artillery as a driver of AEC Matadors in Malta and Libya. He returned to MWM and soon had the PSV licence. By 1956, the effect of the rapidly expanding car ownership was already taking place. The company was too large and scaling down was a painful experience for everyone.

Harold opted to leave in 1961 and went to work for Albert Weaver who had a garage on the Dolfor Road as well as three buses and one minibus. Albert retired in 1966 and Harold purchased the company. The core business would become school contracts plus excursions at the weekends. Beadles was the first company from Newtown to venture abroad to France and Germany. The peak number of buses/coaches must have been 13 coaches and three minibuses. A 53-seat Ford Estoril was purchased for the long distance work. The company was already taking customers to Whitchurch or Shrewsbury for Salopian Tours so Harold decided to see if such tours were viable from Newtown.

The basis of operation was, and remains, the skilled purchase of second-hand buses and extending their lives. The bigger companies received bus grants by the 1970s and this led to units being cascaded down to the second-hand market. There was often a surplus of both double- and single-deck buses that may be too large for Mid-Wales duties. School contracts were often done with a coach so that the same vehicle could be used for evening, weekend and holiday duties. A stage route bus designed for urban use was not comfortable for leisure hire duties.

Harold returned to MWM in 1980 as a Director when the two companies merged to make better use of facilities. The Managing Director, John Griffiths, opted to retire in 1989. Both Owens of Oswestry and Evans of Aberystwyth competed and the higher bid was received from the 'Aber' company. Harold decided to return to his own independent company and rented the Canal Yard for a period of time and then purchased both house and yard on the Middle Dolfor Road.

Harold's wife had now retired from teaching and she set up the business under the brand name of Brenda's Travel Bureau. The basis was that the school

Standard Bedford SB with Duple Super Vega body sold in volume in the late 1950s. The coach had recently been re-sprayed in the late 1960s in Beadles' colours of green and cream.

Harold Beadles Collection

A Bedford with a Yeates body was all chrome as if the company wanted a copy of a USA model.

Harold Beadles Collection

Above: The Weavers yard was beside the embankment and the Dolfor Road railway bridge. Roy Poston is stepping down from the Bedford OB. The need for feeder routes from the isolated hill valleys rapidly increased as the small village schools closed. The Bedford CA van was soon adapted to be a very successful minibus with bench seats in the rear.
Harold Beadles Collection

Left: The open-topper Leyland Atlantean was purchased for special events. It was intended to operate a tourist tour around the historic areas of Shrewsbury. This shows the trial run with the town crier outside the Abbey. The concept was not viable and the bus was sold on. Harold was caught one summer evening in a cloudburst and water cascaded down the stairs like a dam overspill.
Harold Beadles Collection

Bedford AOR 631A is likely to be a YRQ chassis with a variation of a Plaxton Elite body. It is parked on the sea front at Aberystwyth. This was and remains a very popular excursion run. The excursion traffic after 1990 was marketed as 'Brenda's Travel'. Brenda, Harold's wife, stands by the front door. *Harold Beadles Collection*

Bedford VPN 6S Plaxton Supreme III stands in the yard smartly turned out after bodywork cleaning. *Harold Beadles Collection*

A Leyland Dominant has been specially prepared for use by officials of the then Mid-Wales Development Board. The coach is parked in a posed position with a new factory in the background on the Mochdre estate at Newtown. *Harold Beadles Collection*

Two Leylands. Williams of Halfway House owned the Cub on the left. The Leyland Lion half-cab was on the allotments at Llanidloes and was a dwelling of sorts for an old man. Harold arranged to remove it and the vehicle was towed to Newtown by a tractor driven by Roy Poston. *Harold Beadles Collection*

Harold did occasionally stray from the Bedford marque in the 1970s. This is an AEC under-floor engine coach for school contract work. It was purchased from Parish of Morda near Oswestry. Ivor Parish recalls that two AECs were originally bought from Lancashire United. They had 35 seats for coach duties and these were replaced with 45 seats for school contract work.

Harold Beadles Collection

An offer came in for the vintage Leyland Lion. It is being strapped down on a low loader ready to leave the Newtown yard. A similar vehicle is shown in operation driven by Tom Higgs of Llanidloes in the Crosville section of this volume in 1926. *Harold Beadles Collection*

British Motor Corporation (BMC) offered several vans and minibuses either as Austin or Morris. It was based on a car chassis and was too bulky so the ride was poor and front wheel tyre wear would go from new to bald in 3,000 miles. *Harold Beadles Collection*

Ford set out to design a van as a van and not an adaptation of a car chassis. The Ford Transit soon became a market leader with various minibus bodies. This would be one of the earlier models. It was and remains a very good vehicle to drive. The Bedford CF and the Leyland Sherpa would be the main competitors for this market. *Harold Beadles Collection*

W. Edwards of Denbigh was the grandfather of John Jones. The company traded as Red Dragon Motor Service and was sold to Crosville in 1930. John's father and several brothers started a garage in Llanrwst and then 'Dad' purchased Grooms of Newtown just after World War II. The bus is a GMC (General Motors Coach) imported from the USA and was a precursor of Bedfords along with the Chevrolet. The picture stands proudly in the main office at Newtown.

John Jones, Newtown

The Austin CXB coach was supplied new to Car Contracts of London in 1950. Harold Beadles of Newtown purchased the Austin as a reserve coach around 1975 after it had several owners in Kent. It was to stand outside for a number of years. John Jones of Grooms purchased the Austin around 1981 and used his workshop staff to restore the vehicle on quiet days. It then carried out some publicity work with the then Mid-Wales Development Board before being sold to a vintage coach company. The owners in 2005 are Retro Ceremiewagens of Belgium. The bus is shown in Grooms yard just after completion of restoration. *John Jones, Newtown*

contract would use coaches and drivers from 8.00 to 9.30 am and 3.00 to 5.00 pm. A whole range of options developed using capacity during the day, during the evening at weekends and throughout school holidays. These included shopping trips to Shrewsbury, Wrexham, Chester and Aberystwyth giving up to four hours in each town. The Shrewsbury service known as the 'whizzer' operates every Wednesday and occupancy is excellent. These services run as advertised on a turn up and pay basis and therefore qualify for pensioner's free passes. The company caters for the cheap and cheerful market. The small shop in the town centre is covered with billboards promoting day trips to venues within travel distance such as Liverpool, Cardiff, the National Exhibition Centre at Birmingham, etc. plus long weekends in London. A range of summer tours is offered. Late night theatre and concerts including tickets are promoted to venues such as Manchester and Birmingham, many local clubs also hire for private tours.

The company operated seven coaches and two minibuses in 2004. This required a core full time staff and a larger reserve of part time drivers.

Harold has always had an interest in vintage vehicles. He has one Leyland Cub KP3 on site that he hopes to restore. It was owned by Williams of Halfway House and became part of the MWM fleet in 1940. The bus was scrapped in 1953 and ended up as a chicken shed on a farm to the west of Newtown. The bus was purchased by Harold for £10. Such a bus was well-engineered and is under cover to keep out the elements. It still has the roof racks and the rear ladder that was important for a rural bus in the 1930s and 40s.

Harold and Brenda retired. Les Skilton is one of the full-time staff and a Newtown lad. He changed the company name to 'Red Dragon'. The recession, plus high fuel costs, impacted on cash flow, so Les sold on and became a driver for Tanat Valley Motors.

The Stratos story

The father of John Jones was a member of an extended family of brothers. They operated a bus service from Ruthin to Rhyl in Dyffryn Clwyd. The service was sold to Crosville during that company's rapid expansion in the 1930s. John was born in 1932 and the family moved from Denbigh to Llanrwst when John was around five years of age. Father and uncles had purchased a garage in Llanrwst. The Newtown garage was bought in 1946 and the family moved to Newtown. The previous owners were called Grooms and this trading name was retained. John started to help in the garage and then did national service in the Royal Electrical and Mechanical Engineers and returned to help his parents in 1953.

The garage was sold in 1956 and they crossed to the opposite side of the road with increased space to set up a motor factor (wholesalers) and this traded as Grooms Industries. The Lucas Agency was taken in 1959 and the business continued to expand. Diesel engine maintenance and heavy recovery vehicles were based on site as the lorry industry expanded. The company worked with Reed & Mallik servicing diesel equipment during the building of the Clywedog dam.

The word 'motorway' had altered between 1937 and 1970s with the building of the motorway system. Mid-Wales Motorways changed to Mid Wales Travel for marketing continental tours. The first coach operated by the Grooms Group had Mid Wales as the name. This was changed to Stratos to avoid any confusion. The coach is in the Netherlands on the way to Dutch bulb fields. *John Jones, Newtown*

The two original Bova Europa and Bova Futura coaches of Stratos parked at Maesmawr Hall, Caersws *circa* 1984. *John Jones, Newtown*

The team and coach prepare to leave Latham Park for cup final day at Cardiff. John Jones of Stratos is standing on the extreme right with blazer and tie. Football and rugby team plus supporters is a value business for the independent companies of Wales. *Newtown AFC*

Stratos Bulas Eurorider on tour in the Netherlands. *John Jones, Newtown*

Caetano 18-seat coach is at Llyn Fyrnwy in North Montgomeryshire. This is a popular excursion route from the West Midlands as coaches can proceed around the total length of the reservoir.
John Jones, Newtown

Eos Touring with DAF engine. This type of coach with full upper length for passengers would be highly unusual in Mid-Wales. It is sometimes seen within British livery but is more common with a European touring company visiting Wales or proceeding through to the Irish ferry ports. Local drivers disliked the low set driving position and found it claustrophobic and lonely. *Eos* means early dawn in Greek and it is a coincidence that *eos* is also the Welsh for nightingale so this coach needs an early start.
John Jones, Newtown

John retained an interest in the bus industry and became a close business and personal friend of J. Sidney Griffiths (Secretary and then Chair of Mid-Wales Motorways). John had both PSV and HGV licences for vehicle recovery purposes. He helped Mr Griffiths to develop UK and European tours taking the first coach abroad in 1970.

The wholesale business had enterprising staff and was proceeding with an occasional managerial decision. John purchased a new coach in 1982 and decided to target the 'quality' niche of European travel. A new coach is always expensive and such a purchase would be unusual for a Mid-Wales company. There was an element of risk with an initial cross-subsidy from the main business. Two further coaches were purchased in 1984 with a franchise to Global Holidays for tours to Austria. Each coach had to be double-manned for drivers. The price of these tours had to reflect the capital and depreciating costs of the coaches plus the quality of the hotels. The concept and the risk were worthwhile and this new section of the business entered into profit. The coaches had sign writing of Mid-Wales and then Grooms International. In 1985 the company produced brochures under the brand name of Stratos and the two previous names ceased. The company expanded to five coaches with a policy of replacing the oldest unit each year. The company had no school contract or stage route work. However, other work was taken on whenever possible with specialist tours, sports teams, choirs etc.

John retired in 1998 and his son, Colin, took on the coach business. They were successful with a Powys County contract to operate a new Newtown town service route with access for the disabled and elderly. This required a low flow entry bus so a new Dennis Dart Pointer was purchased and the usual driver is David Percival. John still continued as a relief driver as necessary for a time on this service.

The Stratos company started to work in partnership with Owens of Oswestry and then the decision was made to sell their share to Owens. Colin moved to become Tour Manager for Shamrock Tours based in Cardiff. The head office is now at Oswestry but a depot is maintained at Newtown and the company also has a travel agency shop in the town that includes ticket purchase and booking facilities for National Express. The Stratos brand name continues on the coaches.

Apprentices and their succession to other local businesses

Mervyn Foulkes left Newtown Technical School at the age of 15 in 1948. He lived in Adfa. He immediately joined Mid-Wales as a five-year apprentice under the supervision of John and George Banks at the Newtown yard. The yard had only recently transferred to the horse repository. Bill Cross was then a fitter/senior driver and was soon to move on to set up his own garage business. Mervyn also learnt many skills from Owain Owen, the Ministry of Transport Inspector. Mr Owen would visit weekly and Mervyn would work with him on brake testing.

The general fitting duties would include that of the first new Sentinel. It gave much trouble so a Sentinel mechanic would come from Shrewsbury as the

Staff at Newtown depot, *circa* 1958. Mervyn Foulkes, Harold Beadles, Geoff Williams and Roy Poston all valued the quality of skill transfer from George and John Banks. No image can be located of George. The three staff members in front of the Bedford OB are Pryce Owen (ex-ticket inspector from late 1940s peak services and now store-man), Geoff Williams and John Banks (workshop manager). This picture reflects a cultural standard of the 1950s as Pryce has a cotton overall and muffler (scarf), Geoff has a boiler suit but John has a tie, a smart trilby hat and almost certainly a worsted suit under his gabardine mackintosh. *Geoff Williams, Kerry*

The Tuesday-only fair day service from Llanfair to Newtown squeezes through the gap left by vehicles outside M.R. Foulkes garage and tyre depot in Adfa in May 2005. *Author*

vehicle had a 12 month warranty. The problem centred on the Ricardo diesel which was prone to overheating, plus many other teething problems. Extra ducts were fitted in the front valance to try and get better cooling. Access to the engine and gearbox was either through taking off the lower right-side valance or through an inspection plate on the bus floor. Access was not easy compared with the other vehicles.

Mervyn was called up to do National Service in the RAF soon after he was twenty. He was still too young to take the PSV licences. On return, Mervyn opted to join H.V. Bowen Quarries on lorry and quarry machine maintenance. Dad had a small bicycle shop with two petrol pumps in the village of Adfa. He was to die suddenly with cancer so Mervyn took on the shop and expanded this to a service garage and a MOT centre. He had to go to Newtown to get a tyre virtually ever day so he decided to stock his own until the tyre business for all types of vehicles became the dominant section of the business.

Succession has now passed to his sons so once again Mervyn is the tea boy! The last apprentice to join in 1948 would be the tea boy and Mervyn inherited this duty from Harold Beadles. Around 1949, the bus company started a canteen. A lady was employed and she also provided a cooked lunch to order. One of the Directors was very fond of quoits and there was a clay pitch behind one of the sheds. The company worked within a tight financial system and Mervyn's free travel finished on the day the apprenticeship was completed. The Bedford OB buses with the entry door close to the driver could operate on a school run with only the driver. The Bedford Duple coaches with the door halfway down the body needed an extra person to open and shut the door etc. for safety reasons. The apprentices would often carry out this duty in the morning and afternoon. A public service conductor registration was not required as the money exchange was between the Education Authority and the bus company. The morning and evening daily bus from Llanfair Caereinion was packed and many had to stand from Bettws to Newtown. Mervyn could not help but notice Beryl Price of Bettws who worked at a men's outfitters at Newtown. Whether a Crossley half-cab or a Bedford OB, either bus gave a comfortable seat to view the young office and shop ladies. The result has been a recently celebrated 50th wedding anniversary so it was a return fare and not a single.

Geoff Williams was a Newtown lad who commenced work with MWM as an apprentice in 1954. This was completed in 1958 and Geoff continued for a further three years with the company. He acquired a PSV licence including the extra for a double decker. He left to join Corfields Plant Hire of Abermule and would often go up to the road building around the periphery of the Clywedog reservoir to carry out repairs. The company was sold to Naylors of Welshpool and Geoff decided to set up his own plant hire and repair business. MWM had sold the horse repository to another company so they rented their requirements back. Geoff rented some of the now surplus building for his plant hire. He would often help with driving the buses as required. Geoff purchased a minibus around 1970 for a specialist contract with the County Council Social Services to take young adults with mobility difficulties to the then new Dr Richards Special Centre. This started an expansion of more contracts including that to the

AEP 712 was a Crossley half-cab bus with exit/entry door in close view of both the driver and conductor. The vehicle would have a spartan interior with grab handles set on seatbacks and several grab poles so eight standing passengers could be accommodated. The works bus left Llanfair at 6.40 am to arrive at Newtown at 7.45 am and returned leaving Newtown at either 5.30 or 6.00 pm. Mervyn would have travelled on the bus daily for his apprenticeship. Note the advertisement on the cantle for London and Manchester Assurance for some extra income. The Crossley had preference over the Guy Gardner 5cylinder diesel on this route because of the severe gradients.
Ivy Evans, Berriew

MHA 798 is a Crossley coach smartly turned out for a premium excursion or relief for the Cardiff Express. The entry/exit door was situated halfway down the body and these doors could be too heavy for an elderly passenger so the driver had to leave his cab and walk round to operate. There were fewer seats and more luggage space. The seats would have been covered with moquette fabric and there were no seat grabs as no standing passengers were permitted. Geoff Williams recalled that the straight six Crossley engine could have valve coke up. The fitter would take off the engine rocker cover, then sit on the bumper and drip oil into the valves with the engine ticking over. It was a skill that could leave the fitter covered in oil mist. The Guy in the background was one of several with the Gardner engine with five cylinders.
Ivy Evans, Berriew

Photographs of his fellow staff of MWM in 1958: Neil Atkinson (apprentice), Harold Beadles (fitter) Les Pugh (an excellent welder who sadly died when young of cancer) and Derek Thomas (driver/fitter). Derek became a director after the death of Reg Meddins. The picture to the left shows Geoff besides David Williams, the then young school leaver apprentice.

(Both) Geoff Williams, Kerry

An early Ford Transit purchased around 1978 stands as a veteran in the Kerry yard. The transition from plant hire to a minibus contract business took several years.

Geoff Williams, Kerry

Daniel, the son, one of the grandchildren, Samuel and Geoff stand in front of the rear of one the LDV Convoys parked in the small workshop of the Kerry yard in 2005. *Author*

Education Authority. He moved to the Kerry yard in 1981. His wife, Ann, gave much clerical help and support.

The company now has nine minibuses and a school car in 2005. All 8-seaters have a hackney licence and all the larger units have a PSV licence. This enables the business to carry out private hire and excursions. All staff are part time except for Geoff and Daniel, his son. Minor fittings and all valeting are done on Kerry premises but major repairs are now done at a local garage. All minibuses are either Ford transits or LDVs and these are the only two marques that he has used including the earlier Leyland Sherpas and Leyland DAFs.

Geoff started to learn his skills in 1954 under the supervision of John and George Banks. Geoff both worked on and drove the Sentinels. The vehicle was driven over the pit. The valance on the right-hand side was taken off to give both space and light. Some of the quick work could be done sitting on a chair. A wooden trestle with slats that was not unlike a traditional coffin bier was used. The fitter then worked on his side with spanners etc. on the head and the injectors. The horizontal engine suffered with upper cylinder lubrication problems and blown gaskets on the upper cylinder head were a frequent problem.

The valance on the left-hand side covered the fuel tank and inspection was less frequent. Geoff would drive both the Sentinels and the double-deck Guys on the Shrewsbury run. The Sentinel with the light body would keep to time and could accelerate quickly through the gears. Some degree of experience was needed with the gear change because of the long linkage. All the Guys with the five-cylinder Gardner engine were slow and ponderous. The design was for an urban bus. Only one had the six-cylinder engine and the difference was marked. This double-decker was collected from South Wales (Swansea area) and Geoff went down with George Banks to collect the vehicle with brother John returning the van to the depot. No one was familiar with the height of the double-decker. There was a carnival in Brecon with pennants and bunting hanging across the street. The misfortune was that the bus collected these and they trailed along the roof until Geoff got George to stop. It was embarrassing to see the upper section festooned with the carnival flags.

A local group called 'The Other Club' purchased a Bedford Duple from MWM in the mid-1960s. Les Bridge and Geoff were the two drivers. The idea was to attend horse and motor races and had a small bar in the rear. The bus became a problem to park. It was purchased for £600 and sold on for restoration for £300. Geoff noticed the same bus in a vintage magazine in the recent past valued around £8,000.

The older buses were constantly going for scrap in the late 1950s. Some were broken down in the yard to get items that could be re-used. A Mr Draper from Liverpool would collect either the metal scrap or the entire vehicle. Most bus frames were of wood and would quickly burn out leaving the metal as scrap. Geoff reflects back on the events of 50 years ago. Pay rates were low as they had to be just above that for farm-workers. Men like the Bank brothers had so much knowledge of bus structure and their engines. Their skill to transfer this knowledge has stood Geoff well for his working life. An affection for the old company is therefore retained with many memories.

Roy Poston started his apprenticeship with the Managing Director, Ted Neale, who still retained a private garage at Sarn. Roy transferred to the Newtown depot in 1956 when the garage was sold so he did one year in a motor vehicle garage and four years with the bus company. The apprenticeship was still 'on the job' training only and day release plus City & Guilds would not start until the early 1960s. Roy gave his notice in 1965 and moved to Manchester Dock Authority to work on cranes, floating docks and lorries. His wage doubled for fewer hours. Roy must have loved Montgomeryshire for he returned to work with his ex-mate, Harold Beadles, around 1967 as fitter/driver and stayed until the merger of Beadles and MWM in the early 1980s. He continued with a

Roy has completed his apprenticeship and has just passed his PSV test at the age of 21. His first allocated trip was Saturday overtime on an excursion to Rhyl. He therefore had a tie, white shirt and pressed trousers following a tradition of smart turnout. *Roy Poston, Newtown*

local haulage company called Woodhouse for several years until contracts with the Milk Marketing Board started to be phased out. Roy returned to MWM from 1985 until the merger with Evans of Penrhyncoch. The new company transferred him to the head depot at Aberystwyth. The workshop had just been re-equipped and was excellent. It was too far to travel each day so he joined Owens of Newtown where the sons were rapidly diversifying from household coal into bulk and heavy haulage. The company had over 45 lorries in 2005 and also offered heavy vehicle repair and this included to the local bus companies. Roy was the workshop supervisor.

Roy was asked to recall the engines that he had to repair in the mid-1950s. One Sentinel (BEP 864) still retained the original indirect injection Ricardo engine. The other three had the factory alteration to direct injection that had slightly less power than BEP 864 when it ran correctly. Ray thought the Ricardo was from an Argentinian licence. These diesels were vertical engines placed in the horizontal position to get space underfloor. Leyland and AEC had their engines at a slight tilt to avoid the problem of sump oil leaking into the upper cylinder causing both overheating and gasket blow. The engine block was a ferrous cast but the gearbox and bell housing were aluminium. The aluminium would crack and the aluminium welding was done by gas as electricity was not then available. This technique was an art with a fine line between success and disaster. The modern oils are a great improvement. It was not easy to make a winter morning start with the then viscous cold sump oil so all Sentinels plus some others had to be towed for a bump start. This was the first duty every morning. The dubious practice of having a small fire under the sump was another technique. The Sentinel body panels were aluminium and were riveted to a circular steel frame. The problem was that the body may have been too light and was constantly shaking itself apart so rivets were constantly being replaced. The brakes were from a servo vacuum pump and two brake runs would leave the driver with little stopping power for about five minutes until the vacuum was replenished. Gearbox change down was therefore used to supplement stopping to reduce vacuum reservoir reduction. The Sentinel sounds a disaster but it was a brilliant design concept. The driving position was excellent and it could really keep pace on a journey providing the driver did not have to brake too often!

The Gardner five-cylinder diesel engines were fitted to all the Guy half-cab single-deckers and to three of the four Guy double-deckers. These engines were strong and robust but at 38 mph were flat out so they were slow. All depots were envious of Welshpool that had the six-cylinder Gardner.

The Dennis buses either had their own diesel engine or a Gardner. The Crossleys had their own diesel. All 'oilers' tended to have slight leaks but the Crossley was the poorest. However the engine was a powerful 'puller'. The coaches were used for excursion traffic and one was certainly used for the Cardiff Express relief.

The sole Daimler diesel was the star. It was linked to a pre-selector box/fluid flywheel. The powerful 8.6 litre CD6 engine would just cruise along with low revs and excellent fuel economy. Young apprentices did not work on this unit except under strict supervision.

The Bedford Duple Super Vega was on tour and parked in York. Note that an underfloor local stage route bus has drawn into the same area. *Roy Poston, Newtown*

A bridge has now replaced the ferry to the Isle of Skye. Roy has just made enough room with the Bedford for the ramps to be lifted. This would have been a tour in the late 1960s. *Roy Poston, Newtown*

All Bedfords were petrol overhead valve OBs, some of 27 hp and others of 28 hp. They were simple and easy to work on. There must have been around eight refurbished engines on the floor. If any Bedford came in with an engine problem, the engine was just whipped out and one of the spares inserted. The problem would then be solved at leisure and the refurbished engine would join the spares queue. Several Perkins P6 units were fitted for economy but vibration on the engine mountings was chronic. The petrol-engined Commer was underfloor front-mounted. The performance was good but fuel economy was terrible. One was fitted with a Bedford 220 diesel engine but this was under-powered and could hardly move up the gradient. A 300 series Bedford diesel engine solved the problem and all Commers were then fitted with these.

Roy worked a period of time with Harold Beadles. The last of the petrol OBs departed in the mid-1970s and the fleet was then virtually all Bedford diesels. The Ford Estoril D series engine could have problems with overheating and the correct cooling check was an essential daily task as the water pump would go immediately. The bulk of the Bedford engines were within the 330D series. Maybe Bedford was slow in realising that the engines that were good in 1970 would be obsolete a decade later as even small independents were spending time on the motorways. Such engines as the Cummins cancelled out the lower price of the Bedford. The Cummins with low revs, high power and fuel economy was just like the Daimler four decades previously.

Roy retains his PSV licence and will drive on occasions as emergency cover. He usually drives for one week of his holiday and in 2005 he drove for Red Dragon (Les Skilton's succession transfer from Harold Beadles) to Margate with trips to Dover, Canterbury etc. and thoroughly enjoys a week as driver/courier in the company of his wife plus 30 others.

The story of young apprentice fitters started on vesting day, 1937, when the then young Bill Cross started his duties with the newly-formed MWM. Richard Bowen left school and started a motor vehicle apprenticeship at the Dulas Garage owned by Bill Cross in 1975. Bill retired in 1979 and the final year was completed with a West Midland company called Charles Clark. Richard opted to move to Harold Beadles within the year as a fitter and took the PSV licence in 1981. Richard then became part of MWM when the company merged and stayed until 1985. Work was then for a haulage company called Woodhouse. The Milk Marketing Board had to cease because of European regulations on a monopoly and redundancy followed as Woodhouse opted out of milk collection transport. Richard returned to Harold Beadles. A move for independent status started with the purchase of a minibus in 1999. The fleet now has four vehicles. They are an 8-seat Transit, 16-seat executive finish Mercedes, 35-seat Volvo and a 49-seat Scania. The work is school contract and private hire. He had the Kerry to Newtown High School run and this was the final school contract by Arriva (ex-Crosville) in this local area.

Richard is still slowly building up the business. All staff are part time including himself as he works flexi-hours with Owens Transport supporting Roy Poston on heavy lorry fitting. His bus maintenance is done at Owens yard. The bus yard is just beside the Dolfor Road railway bridge on the opposite side of the track from Weavers Garage that was the first site for Beadles Coaches in the mid-1960s. It retains the name of 'the old bulk yard'.

Richard Bowen, inheritor of bus/coach skills from Bill Cross, stands by his Central Travel vehicles that have just returned to the yard from the morning school contracts in autumn 2005. The rear of the 25-seat Volvo stands alongside the Ford Transit and the 53-seat Scania.

Author

The Mercedes 16-seat executive is parked in front of the Tourist Information Centre at Newtown. The computer display screen for all Bws Powys stage routes and other information can be seen set in the wall.

Author

A typical Mid-Wales compromise. The Central Travel coach is parked to collect children from the closed school at Bettws to transport them to the area primary school at Tregynon. The coach is on hire to Beadles whose normal coach and driver are on other duties. Taylors coach is owned by Mid Wales Travel and is collecting Further Education students for Coleg Powys. The Mercedes coach is around 20 years of age. Many independents purchase a unit for a final year or so of work and it may not warrant a total livery re-spray. The only change is the ownership detail painted on the lower valance. *Author (2005)*

One of Geoff Williams' minibuses draws out from Aberbechan canal wharf turn with a feeder school contract. There is an aim to restore the canal for navigation and the working terminus may well have to finish at Aberbechan as the final few miles to Newtown have had sections lost to development. *Author (2005)*

A minibus has descended the Foxes Pitch and is about to cross the bridge over the Mochdre brook. The school contract of Geoff Williams will be the only PSV to cross this bridge as the Mochdre stage service of 1950 has long since ceased. *Author (2005)*

The Central Travel Volvo grinds up the gradient of the Vastre hill in the same place as the pre-war Bedford in 1950. Note the expansion of the linear Newtown along the narrow valley except for the flood plain that is parks, sports fields, golf course and a nature reserve. *Author (2005)*

Chapter Four

Celtic Travel of Llanidloes

Llanidloes is the last substantial settlement on the River Severn as the valley closes in before the final climb of the river to the source high on the Pumlumon Mountain. Llanidloes is an attractive small market town with a good tourist base. The best feature may be the market hall. The situation of this hall determines that full length buses have to transverse the by-pass to enter the town from the western junction to avoid the narrow width in the town centre. The railway closed in 1962. The Crosville replacement service to Brecon only ran for about four years. The Llanidloes, Newtown, Shrewsbury stage route is the most frequent service in the county.

The area is surrounded by spectacular scenery including the lakes (technically reservoirs) of the Elan Valley and Clywedog. It has a long history of both wool processing and lead mining. Public transport except to Newtown is sparse, although there has been improvement with connections to Aberystwyth and Rhayader with County/Assembly support in the last few years.

The dominant coach-company of Llanidloes is Celtic Travel; Peter Jones recalls its history. Trevor Jones, Peter's father, founded the bus section of the company in the early 1930s. Trevor had already started car repairs and a taxi service at Llangurig. A purpose-built garage and bungalow was built on the western edge of the village. The forecourt looks straight out on the embankment that was the final few yards of the failed railway with the optimistic hope of arriving at Strata Florida so that Manchester & Milford Railway could have a share of the Irish packet trade. The embankment was a linear play area for the children in the 1940s.

A second-hand Chevrolet was purchased. There were two stage routes: the first ran from Manod near Eisteddfa Gurig to Llanidloes on a Saturday and the second ran to Rhayader and the Elan Valley on a Wednesday. The company joined Mid-Wales Motorways in 1937 and the depot became based in Llanidloes. Both Crosville and MWM worked daily buses to the shadow factories in Newtown during the war. The garage business started to grow with the Rootes Agency (Hillman, Humber, Sunbeam-Talbot and Commer). The bus section became independent from MWM in the late 1950s. Trevor purchased the current workshop/depot from a previous cabinet- maker. Bedford OB BEP 691 came as part payment of the share that Trevor had put in during 1937. The company was called Trevor Jones and Sons and it assumed the name of Celtic Travel when Trevor officially retired. Peter and his wife, Glenda, took on the business. Brian, the other brother, was now in the teaching profession.

School contracts expanded rapidly after 1948 when all 11 plus children came into the secondary schools. Some students travelled by train to Newtown Technical School. All this trade transferred from the railway for the then Further Education College in January 1963 and continues to Coleg Powys to this day. The other trade is tours within the UK and Ireland plus local excursions and private hire.

Trevor Jones joined the MWM group in 1937 and ran the Llanidloes/Llangurig depot. A number of ladies joined the company during World War II. Katie Jones became one of the drivers both for MWM and Crosville. She is seen standing by the radiator of a Bedford WTB. The bus is parked in Llanidloes and the unobscured headlights would indicate that the war had concluded.
Mid Wales Travel Depot, Newtown

Gareth Owen (*left*) and Mike Harris (*right*) stand at the rear of a rebuilt Dennis with body designed for school contracts. They appeared from the pit where they have been checking the brakes. The executive on the right remains in the previous owner's livery and only the sign writing on the lower valance indicate that it is in the ownership of Celtic Travel. *Author (2005)*

High capacity school routes in the 1990s required a double-decker to carry up to 70 pupils. The vehicle parked close to the workshops is a former Eastern National Bristol VRT.

Gareth Owen, Llanidloes

The 70-seat body (with three by two seats plus safety belts) painted in bright yellow has just returned to Trefeglwys Area Primary School from Llanidloes swimming pool at 3.20 pm with driver Phil Evans. This example is on a Leyland chassis. The driver can observe all on the single floor. Entry and exit view is good. The use of double-deck buses in Wales is now subject to scrutiny due to several accidents in South Wales almost certainly caused by student misbehaviour.

Author (2005)

A single-deck bus body on a Bedford YMT chassis was not common with independents. This is a Duple Dominant. It had a good reputation with some of the smaller municipal fleets. The bus has just had full overhaul for school contract work (*circa* late 1980s). *Gareth Owen, Llanidloes*

Volvo B10M and Volvo Van Hool parked close to the workshop after or awaiting inspection in a section of the public car park. The majority of the fleet is parked in the Smithfield Yard. The 'Trewythen Arms' is in the background. The yard of this old coaching inn was the short-lived Crosville depot in 1924 and then the Crosville parking area before World War II. *Author (2005)*

This strange looking bus was a custom order for the then new Powys Education Authority in 1974. It was almost certainly with a 300 cubic inch petrol engine on SB chassis officially designated as NFM for export. Diesels would have 100 per cent of the home market by this date. The special body kit was assembled by Celtic Travel with bench seats and was austere: the experiment was not a success. Gareth does not know what happened to these buses but they would have been totally uneconomic in the UK without a diesel engine.

Gareth Owen, Llanidloes

A Bedford YMT with Plaxton Supreme body has had a full overhaul and been re-sprayed in Celtic Travel livery. This second-hand coach is now is pristine condition (*circa* late 1980s).

Gareth Owen, Llanidloes

The Celtic Travel coach is seen at 3.50 pm from the disused track of the Van railway on school contract to Van, Staylittle and Dylife. The coach is crossing the River Cerist and the bank edge still shows signs of lead pollution. The renovated Garth crossing keeper's cottage and station remnants can be seen. The station had seen its last passenger train in 1879. The coach will turn left and head up through the village and the lead mine relicts. It may be the only place where a Van Hool will be seen passing the Van Pool (reservoir for the lead works). *Author (2005)*

Trevor Jones operated a stage route on Wednesday/Saturday only to Elan Valley and Rhayader prior to World War II. The Rhayader Royal Mail Post Bus calls at the Elan Valley Visitor Centre at 1.15 pm between April and October only. It will arrive at Rhayader Post Office at 1.20 pm and then take a further 75 minutes to travel via various communities to Llandrindod. *Author (2004)*

The Crossgates low-floor Optare leaves Rhayader Dark Lane car park at 1.30 pm and will arrive at Llandrindod railway station via the direct route at 1.56 pm. The station car park in Llandrindod is central and convenient for the main shops, museums and hotels as well as having rail connections to Swansea and Shrewsbury. *Author (2004)*

The G3A Crossgates Dennis waits to depart from Rhayader at 2.15 pm to arrive at Llanidloes at 2.35 pm travelling via Dernol & Llangurig. The G designation is given to services funded by the Welsh Assembly to try and improve travel between towns. *Author (2004)*

The Central Grammar School, Birmingham had a camp at Bryn-tail near Llanidloes and this started to operate in the late 1910s. Students are waiting to depart from Llanidloes station to Birmingham (Snow Hill) in the clerestory-roofed carriages of the Cambrian or GWR.

Brian Hutton, Birmingham

The rail passenger services were withdrawn from Moat Lane to Llanidloes and beyond in December 1962. A coach hired from Stockland of Birmingham unloads students and their luggage in the Clywedog valley in 1968. The road changed from an accommodation lane to a new B road so that tourist coaches can travel on the eastern flank of the new reservoir. The Post Bus and school bus still take the detour via the Van village. *Brian Hutton, Birmingham*

The current fleet has 16 coaches including four executives and four minibuses. The company now has five 70-seat (3x2) yellow coaches purchased from the Bristol Bus and Coach Company who fitted the school bus on either an older Dennis Javelin or Leyland chassis. Such coaches follow a USA concept and Peter thought that both Dennis and Volvo had new coaches for specific school transport. However, the price of providing such new buses must rise if the political decision is made to choose to have a dedicated school bus.

Four bodies were assembled on the Bedford chassis with petrol engines in 1974 for the then new Powys Education Authority. The experiment was not judged a success and these buses certainly needed a diesel engine. The company has only ever purchased one new bus for its own use and that was a Bedford SB3 (CEP 262). Currently, there are three full-time office workers, two full-time fitters and two full-time drivers. All others are part time. The company has retained both full-time and part-time staff for many years.

Other companies have operated in the area in the past. Monty Morgan ran an independent service with a Commer 29-seater in the 1950s. A Mr Davies had and still retains several coaches at Pant-y-dŵr. Mantles of Trefeglwys also operated several buses for a number of years and still has minibus feeders into the area primary school of Trefeglwys. The Bumfords also had a Bedford OB at Trefeglwys. Ted Morris has a Bedford OB at Llandinam and Bradleys had a Bedford CF as a school feeder in the late 1960s.

Some of the accompanying photographs are from Gareth Owen. Both Gareth and Mike Harris have worked with the company since the 1960s starting under the tutelage of Trevor Jones. They are skilled fitters, welders and bodywork repairers. Both have a PSV licence to help out with the morning and afternoon school contract. Peter acknowledges that such men are the backbone of an independent. They keep older high mileage vehicles to the necessary operating standard. Gareth recorded many of the coaches with his camera as they completed a full refit in the workshops.

The administrative office of Coaching Connection is based in Llanidloes. The company offers a range of long distance tours on the continent. The Kassbohrer Setra is parked at Y Gro in Llanidloes. The coach is owned by Roberts Coaches of Aberystwyth so this is a joint venture. *Author (2004)*

The MWM Bedford OB is within the Mochdre Brook Gorge between Mochdre and the open hill of Pentre Chapel returning to Newtown. It has just crossed the bridge and will have to grind up a gradient on severe curves. It is thought that the driver was Cyril Haines. The photograph was taken in 1970. Messrs Weavers may have started the service and then Neales before entering the MWM timetables in 1937. The service operated on Tuesdays and Saturdays with some terminating at Mochdre and only a few going on to the scattered community centred at Pentre Chapel.

A. Moyes, Aberystwyth/Wyn Lloyd's Collection

Chapter Five

Lloyds Coaches of Machynlleth

Machynlleth is unique in Powys as it is situated just above sea level. The historic hamlets grew into a town with a focus for traffic especially as the lowest crossing point of the Afon (River) Dyfi. The section of the trunk road across the flood plain will still flood for several hours when a high spring tide coincides with the river in full spate. Sometimes this is just inconvenient but it can also be severe. The Montgomeryshire seashore is a muddy saline bank on the southern side of the estuary close to the railway track heading to Dyfi Junction station. Derwenlas would have been a coastal shipping point for lime in and lead ore out. The town has a number of architectural features of value. There are several buildings from the late medieval period including the parliament house of Owain Glyndŵr. The central focal point is the clock tower. The entry into the yard of several hotels will immediately show relics of the coaching industry. The renovated station is larger than expected as the Newtown & Machynlleth Railway (1863-1869) intended it to be both workshops and offices. It was absorbed into the Cambrian Railways and the railway sheds covered much of the needs of the coastline railway to Pwllheli. The Corris narrow gauge station and exchange yard adjoins this complex. The bus station may be one of the best of those designed by R.C. Cowmeadow in the 1930s as many were knocked down for redevelopment in the 1980s transfer to private companies. Cowmeadow was the internal architect for Crosville and his designs are readily identifiable.

There can be no doubt that Machynlleth has the best public transport access in the Montgomeryshire area. This is exploited by locally-produced pamphlets for tourists and locals and gives full details of train and bus services. The area has an expanding facility for cycling including many mountain bike routes especially with forestry access roads. Many of the tourist attractions have access to train or bus stage routes including the coastal areas at Borth, Ynyslas, Aberdyfi and Tywyn. Ynyshir Nature Reserve, Furnace Iron Mill (CADW), the Tywyn and Corris narrow gauge railways, craft workshops and the King Arthur Caves at Corris and finally the Centre for Alternative Technology all have stage route access. Attractions within the town are all close to the station and bus stops and include the Modern Art Gallery, y Plas, the leisure centre and a wide range of shops.

Some early bus services were within the operation of both the Corris Railway and the GWR and these were absorbed into Western Transport and then Crosville in the early 1930s. Independents may have played a lesser role than other parts of the county because of the geographical site of Machynlleth as a natural rural hub for transport over the centuries.

Wyn Lloyd is a local man. He started his career as an agricultural engineer at the then Montgomery College of Further Education at Newtown in 1979. One of his staff tutors would have been the author. He then joined MWM at their Newtown depot. He would have completed his apprenticeship within the

A Crosville Bristol and a Mid-Wales Motorways AEC are parked together in the Horse Repository yard at Newtown. Crosville used the yard for daily valets, fuel check and overnight parking but the bus would have received full service at Crosville Oswestry depot. The photograph was taken on a Saturday in April 1971. A Crosville bus also worked the shifts at the then BRD factory during the week. This factory was the wartime shadow factory that generated much bus business between 1940 and 1945 over three shifts.

A. Moyes, Aberystwyth/Wyn Lloyd's Collection

LFA 31 is on the ramp at Mid-Wales Motorways yard for inspection. Geraint Gittins of Dolanog was the owner of this vehicle and he may have used the facilities at the depot during a wait of three hours plus at Newtown with a school visit to such a venue as the Oriel Art Gallery.

A. Moyes, Aberystwyth/Wyn Lloyd's Collection

Two MWM Bedford OBs and three Crosville Bristols share space at the Smithfield Cattle Market at Welshpool in June 1971. The auctioneers hired the space for overnight parking, cleaning etc. on the condition that there was no bus on site on Monday market day. The nearest Bristol was purchased from Red & White of Chepstow. The site had pressure-washers etc. for market lorries. *A. Moyes, Aberystwyth/Wyn Lloyd's Collection*

The Bristol KG161, registration LFM 742 was new in 1950. It has rear entry/exit for passengers and was only suitable for conductor operation. The Machynlleth to Dinas Mawddwy bus route started in 1924 and competed with the light railway until closure in 1931. The Tilling Group used a Bristol chassis with the body by Eastern Coach Works and Gardner engine for most vehicles from 1945 until the creation of National Bus Company in 1970. A Moyes thinks that the print may have been from R.H.G. Simpson. *Wyn Lloyd's Collection*

The Bristol SC4LK became available for Crosville from 1957. It was designed for one-man rural operation. The bus is at Abercegir and the only service in 2009 is a daily Lloyds midibus. Some of the more rural routes from Machynlleth (and also Oswestry and Aberystwyth) were generous beyond any realistic hope of income. One retired driver had the opinion that it was difficult to take a car on some of these upland lanes, let alone a bus.

A. Moyes, Aberystwyth/ Wyn Lloyd's Collection

The Bristol (and the photograph) both date from the 1960s and was an example of the Lodekka to maintain capacity with reduced height. The bus depot is at Machynlleth and was designed by Crosville's architect in the 1930s. It may now be the best remaining example of design from R.C. Cowmeadow.

Wyn Lloyd

motor vehicle trade with much emphasis on diesel engines and commercial electrical systems. He left the company at Newtown to become a driver for Crosville Motors at Machynlleth when the company was part of the National Bus Company. The company asked him if he would transfer to the Dolgellau depot as the fitter and relief driver. Wyn returned to Machynlleth within the privatised-company of Crosville Cymru and he became the traffic supervisor for South Gwynedd and North Powys. This would have included the period when a depot started at Abermule. Wyn transferred to Arriva Cymru and remained with them until 2001 when he set up his own bus company. He started within the old station yard of Corris Railway with everything outside. Wyn took the opportunity to purchase the Crosville depot and the trading address retains the name of the Old Crosville Garage. He therefore operates from the only purpose-built bus garage in Montgomeryshire.

The core business is stage services and school contracts for both Powys and Gwynedd, general coach hire for the local community and rail replacement duties. The geographical position of Machynlleth with both the coastline and the main Cambrian railway line generates much hire, often at very short notice.

The fleet at April 2005 consists of six large coaches, four of these are Volvos and the two oldest are Leylands plus five midi 29-seaters, all of which are Mercedes 709s. Wyn employs nine full-time drivers and fitters and has a pool of six part-time drivers. Certain services sponsored by Bws Gwynedd required a common livery, otherwise all buses are in a livery of silver, red and yellow.

The school contract from Machynlleth consists of three Lloyds buses to Dinas Mawddwy, Aberllefenni and Ceinws. A Mid Wales Travel bus based at Newtown heads out to Carno and was also the works bus for the Laura Ashley factory. The then April 2005 stage routes were 518 (Machynlleth to Dinas Mawddwy), 521 Machynlleth town service, 30 Tywyn, Abergynolwyn and Minffordd*, 28 Llanegryn to Machynlleth, 29 Clipa Tywyn town service and alternate Saturdays limited stop from Machynlleth to Chester via Tywyn, Dolgellau, Bala, Corwen, Llangollen and Wrexham. (This follows much of the closed Barmouth to Ruabon line with the Llangollen/Corwen section now an heritage railway.) Both Powys and Gwynedd county councils have since added extra subsidised services.

Historically there was a GWR bus so walkers could reach the Cader Idris area for mountain climbing. It may be worthwhile to consider a Sherpa equivalent (Sherpa operates around Snowdonia) for access to Cader Idris and also Machynlleth, Dylife, Llanidloes bus so walkers have access to the Glyndŵr long distance footpath.

Both the main Cambrian and coast railway routes are single track with passing places. Short notice bus replacement is needed with such examples as flooding usually at Welshpool, Caersws or the Dyfi estuary, breakdowns, etc. but also late running. One problem is congestion at Birmingham (New Street). The Aberystwyth train can terminate at Wolverhampton to reduce this problem. Passengers can be moved either on Virgin's services or the London Midland suburban trains. Trains can also be curtailed at Machynlleth so that coaches are necessary to complete the journey to and from Aberystwyth. Pre-

* There was a previous promotion with a special bus from Abergynolwyn via Corris to Machynlleth so summer visitors could travel a circular route from Machynlleth to Tywyn on the standard gauge and then travel from Tywyn to Abergynolwyn on the narrow gauge. This journey can still be done on the stage route.

The clock tower in the background is an important feature of Machynlleth. YFM 282L was delivered in 1973 and is working route 18. Financial help from Gwynedd County Council started by the mid-1980s and the bus had a Gwynedd County Council red front. Dinas Mawddwy is just over the border in the old county of Merionydd. These were some of the first buses shopped out in National Bus Company livery but they were a composite bus/coach design for rural areas.

A. Moyes, Aberystwyth/Wyn Lloyd's Collection

Coach loading takes place at the end of the school day outside Newtown High School in May 1978. All buses are from Mid-Wales Motorways. One of the last of the OBs (BEP 882), now at least 28 years of age, hides a Bedford VAM as a Bedford Duple heads out to Kerry.

A. Moyes, Aberystwyth/Wyn Lloyd's Collection

Coaches start arriving for the end of the school day at Machynlleth High School. The first of three of Wyn Lloyd's coaches is behind the Mid Wales Travel coach for Carno. This bus, based at Newtown, dovetails into the works bus duty for the Laura Ashley factory at Carno. Roy Poston recalls that demand was so great in the late 1970s that a double-deck bus was needed for the factory work staff.

Author (2005)

Leyland National GMA 399N was delivered to Crosville in 1974 when it was within the National Bus Company (NBC). GMA was used as part of a sequence to register vehicles at Chester on a new computer system. The bus is at Pen-y-cob terminus at Aberllefenni further up the Dulas valley from Corris. Aberllefenni was the last station of the Corris railway. A further contour and incline tramway continued from this point to the Ratgoed slate quarry and the trace can be observed running just above and to the right of the bus roofline.

A. Moyes, Aberystwyth/Wyn Lloyd's Collection

The view is the Aberystwyth station forecourt bus exchange. The bus is an Arriva Midlands North with display for Harlescott Park and Ride that is on the eastern side of Shrewsbury. It is thought that the vehicle may have been Abermule-based and was at Aberystwyth for use on an Arriva internal service arrangement.

Wyn Lloyd, Machynlleth

Wyn chose to start outside in the corner of a garden centre in 2001. The area was once the exchange siding of the Corris Railway. The Crosville garage became part of an asset of a lease company and ceased to be used for buses. Arriva leased it back as storage in the late 1990s as most of the garage equipment had been stripped out. Wyn acquired the premises and invested with necessary equipment so both he and his staff now have reasonable conditions for coach repair. The yard is now used for bus/coach storage as the business expands. The yard and the bus depot are only about 300 metres either side of Machynlleth railway station. The photograph therefore could be within either Arriva/Crosville or Lloyds Coaches periods as Wyn would have worked here in the late 1990s. *Wyn Lloyd, Machynlleth*

Three Mercedes 709s are parked on the forecourt of the 'Old Crosville Garage'. The drivers are having a break and soon one bus will work the Machynlleth town service and another will leave for the mid-day Dinas Mawddwy Wednesday-only extra service. *Author (2005)*

The mid-day service 518 enters the village of Aberangell. The trees are on the embankment of the Dinas Mawddwy Light Railway that was lifted in the early 1950s. The bus has just passed the site of a low bridge that was dismantled in the late 1960s to enable lorries and double-deck buses to enter the village. *Author (2005)*

Buses parked in the yard of the old Corris railway at Machynlleth. One old midi is being held for spare parts. Both the Plaxton and the double-deck bus show the Frazer Eagle Rail replacement logo and hire number. The double-decker is an ex-West Midland Travel MCW Metro-rider and was hired for the five weeks when the Ffriog coastline section of the railway needed repair caused by wave erosion. The bus was needed for High School carriage from Tywyn to Barmouth and Harlech. There is still train hire for schools because of the shorter route of rail across the estuary-bridge to Barmouth. *Author (2005)*

Wyn Lloyd has just driven the Volvo B10M to Machynlleth station ready for the rail replacement 3.30 pm to Pwllheli on 13th April. Note Frazer Eagle sign to the right of the school bus symbol. This was during the period when the Ffriog rail track had to be repaired because of wave damage. *Author (2005)*

The Volvo B10M draws under the low bridge by the railway station between Lloyds Garage and the coach park. The river will flood from under the bridge across the ½ mile of flood plain seen through the bridge. This can cause traffic disruption, especially for cars, for several hours until the combination of high spring tide and river flood recede. *Author (2005)*

The tender for the Machynlleth-Newtown service for Bws Powys was awarded to Lloyds Motors in August 2005. The Optare Tempo parked outside the Old Crosville Garage is the first new bus purchased by the company. The Tempo has the six-cylinder 906LA Mercedes Benz engine. This is an innovative experiment to see if a new unit with low noise level, easy access and comfort of service can tempt additional passengers from their cars. The service is part of a long-term plan for better rail and coach connections over a longer interval of the day. It now integrates with the Newtown-Brecon-Merthyr Tydfil experiment for connections to Cardiff commencing in 2006.

Author (2005)

The Lloyd's Optare Tempo waits to leave Newtown at 9.15 am for the return to Machynlleth on a Saturday morning. It takes its place at the bus station bay. The coach and buses read as follows *from left to right*: Celtic Travel on an excursion pick up, Arriva Midland North to Shrewsbury, Mid Wales Travel town service, Lloyds and finally the Crossgate morning service to Llandrindod Wells.

Author (2005)

planned hire work takes place with engineering works especially at weekends. Wyn was working a special contract for five weeks in April 2005. Wave erosion into a cave collapsed part of the line at Ffriog between Fairbourne and Llwyngwril. This section of line has a rock shelter and engines have been swept off twice since 1865. Wyn had to operate a service replacement and hire an additional double-decker for the school services between Tywyn, Barmouth and Harlech. All rail hire services were contracted to Fraser Eagle Management Services and not the train operator. The coach would be identified with the Fraser Eagle banner and may also have the additional train company banner. An executive coach, with a toilet, would be requested, if available. The hire was for rail travel replacement only with drop off and pick-up points only at stations. Only relevant train staff could accept money and issue tickets. Vehicles were expected to have clean interior/exterior and the driver must wear corporate uniform if available or wear shirt with tie. (None of the local independents has a corporate uniform.)

Wyn and other operators are faced with the added problem on these services of items such as bikes, prams and wheel chairs that are difficult to accommodate, make entry/egress slower, and with large luggage takes time to load and unload. Often the station yard had no canopy and is being battered with Welsh rain. In addition, passengers are often stressed due to late running so a degree of comfort and care is required from the driver who may also just have lost his evening of leisure. Both Wyn and other companies have to tender for much of their work and the future pattern may alter. Obviously Wyn knew that negotiations were proceeding for him to have Bws Powys support for operating the Newtown-Machynlleth prime route and his tender was successful and operation with a brand new Optare Tempo started in August 2005.

Wyn offered a substantial number of photographs for selection. They cover his time with MWM, Crosville, Arriva Cymru and his own independent company. A number are from Anthony Moyes of Aberystwyth. However, identification of source may have errors as Wyn found several prints within old files. Anthony Moyes has written several books on the history of buses and has also written many essays for various bus magazines, especially those concerned with the Welsh companies. He gives the following details of the rail-related buses. The first local Corris railway bus was Machynlleth to Aberhosan starting on 13th February, 1922 (this was a failed 1919 proposal from the County Council for a light railway extension). Further services started between February and May 1924 between Machynlleth and Newtown, Machynlleth and Tywyn and finally to Dinas Mawddwy. The Mawddwy Light Railway passenger service continued until 1931. The GWR started a road service between Machynlleth and Aberystwyth. All, plus GWR bus services at Welshpool, were absorbed into Western Transport and then became part of Crosville in 1933. Crosville started a Machynlleth-Llanwrin service in 1935.

The Jehus and the Astleys were pre-World War I motor engineers that did not invest in post-war buses. The surname of Jehu is not uncommon in Montgomeryshire. There is an expression in Welsh of *'mynd fel Jehu'* that translates as 'going like the clappers'. Jehu and his chariot appear in the Bible in Kings II and Jehu said: 'If you are on my side, see that no one escapes from the city to tell the news in Jezreel'. One wonders if Llewelyn Jehu would have got his 1913 Model T Ford as far as Welshpool. *The Powysland Club (Copyright Dr W.T.R. Pryce of Cardiff)*

Plenydd Gittins is at the wheel of his charabanc ready to take some people from the Dolanog area on an excursion. Such rural outings in the 1920s opened up a new horizon. *Geraint Gittins*

Chapter Six

Llanfair Caereinion and the Surrounding Area

Llanfair Caereinion is the smallest of the towns with a High School catchment area. The town (or village) is on the Banwy River and the valley opens up into a wide vale downstream towards Meifod.

There are a number of small settlements along the Upper Banwy but much of land is that of high sheep walks and moors with some forest plantation and only a few isolated settlements. It would seem unbelievable that the Mid-Wales Motorways had a market day only service starting at Gosen in Cwm Nant-yr-eira in the 1940s. The town attracts many visitors interested in transport as it has the head office, café/ bookshop and workshops for the narrow gauge heritage Welshpool Llanfair Railway. Transport routes date back to Roman times as the valley was one route that radiated from Viroconium (Wroxeter) east of Shrewsbury. There is evidence of early British settlements and several of the very attractive small ancient churches may well be on earlier pagan sites. It is certain that many of the bridges are on or close to fords. The turnpike from Welshpool through Llanfair and Dinas Mawddwy to the coast would have been more important than that through Newtown before the canal and railway era. This area was not, and still is not, a rich picking for a bus stage route.

Llanfair has been the most difficult area to provide a visual record of any bus activity before World War II. David Mills Evans, often called Leon, attempts his explanation. David's mother's family came from the Van area and he has some stories of the lead mine branch line from Caersws to the Van. His grandmother recalled that a fatality was brought out on the tramway and taken down the incline for the family to identify. He supposed a modern visit to a mortuary would be equally traumatic. Mills is a name associated with hymn writing in Welsh in the Victorian period from the Llangurig/Llanidloes area.

David was born in 1927 and has lived in the Llanfair area apart from service with the Royal Navy in the late 1940s. He has become one of several locals who seek to collect valued details of the past community. His interest has been the turnpike roads and the horse transport prior to World War I. Llanfair people had made much effort to secure the narrow gauge light railway opened in 1905 and retained a loyalty to it. This factor may have held back bus development with the town. A Mr Astley owned a small Dixie * (charabanc) used for local leisure trips. The GWR started to supplement the train with its own bus using Welshpool staff. The service was taken over by Western Transport and then Crosville in quick succession in the early 1930s. Crosville formed Leon's earliest memory of a bus trip on the daily pre-war bus to Welshpool. Crosville also operated a bus to Oswestry via Meifod. Several villages had local buses including Gittins of Dolanog. David John Arthur of Llanerfyl had a bus route from the Foel to Llanfair. His company merged with MWM. The yard for the

* Dr W.T.R. Pryce has published *The photographer in Rural Wales* centred on Llanfair Caereinion. He confirms the existence of Astley's charabanc used for fairs, church and chapel trips. His father hired the charabanc for a seaside day out for the family and friends at Borth.

The Welshpool & Llanfair light railway was struggling for passengers in the late 1920s and the service closed in 1931. The GWR had operated a mixed goods and passenger service with steam power but used the more economic bus to supplement the service. The bus went further up the valley to Y Foel and over the watershed to Dinas Mawddwy. The driver would have been one of the two Rowland brothers based in Welshpool. This bus worked a shuttle from Abermule to Kerry for three Fridays in August/September to move dealers and buyers for the Kerry Hill Sheep sales. The Kerry branch was congested with sheep wagons. *National Railway Museum*

The same view in May 2005 at Llanfair Caereinion as Megan Jones moves Allen Watkin's coach from the yard for the school contract from Llanfair to Y Foel. Note the cars parked on double yellow lines leaving little room for the coach to squeeze through. *Author*

buses moved to a site on the Newtown Road by the Cefn Coch turning. David had little experience of MWM travel as the bus routes centred on collecting people from Cefn Coch, Adfa, New Mills and Manafon so they left Llanfair with few people but filled up on the stage route. D.J. Arthur's bus became very popular in the late 1930s on Saturday evenings for the Welshpool cinema. The stage routes started to be withdrawn from the 1960s as car ownership became common. Llanfair was left with a very poor service. MWM closed its depot in 1963 and the local taxi driver, Selwyn Hughes, filled the vacuum with school contracts and excursion business. MWM drivers such as Vernon Evans and John James appear elsewhere in this history. The late Dic Williams was the foreman at the MWM yard.

Leon has several interesting transport stories. His bungalow is beside the rail track and his purchase inherited the right to cross the track. The pre-war GWR asked for 5*s*. per annum rent for the gate and the crossing to a strip of land by the river. A large tree was starting to overhang the property and a letter was written to British Railways in the early 1950s. A reply came from Wolverhampton with the suggestion that David could arrange for the tree to be cut down and use the result for firewood. This was done and then it was found that the tree was not on BR property but on the edge of the local farm field.

David John Arthur

Nest Davies, née Pierce-Roberts, has kindly written her recall of David John Arthur and his buses. A précis of the translation now follows. Everyone called him Davy John or Dafi Jon. Davy John worked as a saddler at Talafon, Llanerfyl and he started a garage with car sales and repair in the 1920s. Bob Francis of Foel had a charabanc in the early 1920s but he did not develop any stage routes. His business was that of excursions to the seaside and social events. Certainly Davy John's bus was taking children to the County School at Llanfair. It is believed that he tried to persuade the Traffic Commisioners to share the Crosville route as his daily stage route was only from the Foel to Llanfair where passengers could connect with Crosville for either Welshpool or Oswestry. There was a morning bus, another around lunchtime and another around teatime. There was a special late bus on Saturdays for the cinema at Welshpool. The Monday market bus was allowed to work through to Welshpool. Nest started to travel on the bus to the County School in 1935. The Monday bus was overloaded with school children, adults, eggs etc. One sedate old lady always called the children 'the kind ones' as seats would be given up to the older people. Health and Safety regulations were different then. Sometimes the bus was truly full to the brim. Some of the children would climb up the rear ladder and hold on inside the railings of the roof. It was a lovely way to return home on a warm summer day!

Maybe Davy John had three buses and therefore several drivers. Nest is not certain when Davy John retired but he did continue to drive in the war years with MWM.

The war came with chronic shortage of petrol. One morning a strong smell went through the bus and every child put on their gas mask. The truth was that

Above: Davy John Arthur's bus may be parked in the background of this view at Llanerfyl. Gareth's mother is the young lady. The photograph would date from the mid-1930s. Everyone is in best clothes so it may have been a Sunday school trip. *Gareth Evans, Llanfair Caereinion*

Right: Davy John Arthur was a cousin to Bernice's father. This is the only photograph that Bernice and her cousins can locate.
Bernice Jones, Aberhafesb

Below: The three lads stand in front of the MWM Bedford Super Vega at Blackpool. The date would be the late 1950s and the coach would have left the Llanfair depot earlier that day. It is a coincidence that a Marcher Vega from Ludlow is in the adjoining parking space.
Gareth Evans, Llanfair Caereinion

the petrol had been diluted with some paraffin so the fuel combustion was not good. Soon afterwards some of the lads composed a song and the verses became popular and were written down.

Mae llawer math of fysys	There are many types of buses
Yn myned trwy y fro	going through the area
Mai rhai yn mynd ar betrol	Some go on petrol
A'r lleill ar TVO	And some on TVO
Mae gan a saddler fysys	The saddler has buses
Sy'n mynd ar baraffin	That go on paraffin
A rhaid cael bechyn cryfion	Must have strong lads
I'w gwthio yn eu tin	To push it at the rear
Mae'n rhaid cael Bili Arnold	Must have Billy Arnold
I moen y bali scrap	To take it for scrap
Mae'n well gan bobl hastus	It is better to those in a hurry
Gael poni bach a thrap	To have a small pony and trap

(TVO is tractor vaporising oil that was a paraffin or kerosene with a dye added for tractor use only. The tractor had a special manifold that vaporised the fuel for ignition. Billy Arnold. Every area had a scrap merchant as metal scrap had a good value for war needs.)

Another problem was the very cold weather. Davy John did his best to get the Upper Banwy children to the grammar school. One day, the radiator froze and Davy stopped at a farm and got some hay. This was lit under the engine until Davy decided to venture on to school. Suddenly steam came out of the blown radiator and Davy stood on the seat to try and see above the steam. The buses were nicknamed as 'the coffee pots'. The children all got to school and no accident was ever recorded. Davy was a lovely man and the district was lucky to have him.

Nest was a teenage girl in the war. She would not have known the make of buses or any other technical feature. Davy John had a small family but she thought that they left the area to seek work elsewhere and tracing any family would now not be easy. His limited service played a vital role within the Upper Banwy Valley in the 1920s and 1930s until he merged into Mid-Wales Motorways.*

Margaret Brett (née Brett) was an evacuee from Liverpool and stayed with the Arthurs during 1940/41. Margaret remembers the three buses. There were two employees, both called Dai bws and certainly one was Dai Puw or Pugh. Margaret was astonished at the contrast with Liverpool. The grammar school children cycled in from the isolated holdings to pick up points. Margaret travelled on the Monday only during holidays when the bus was laden with farm produce. On return, she would help Huw (the son) count the takings that were tipped on the kitchen table and also fill the ticket rack for the next day. Margaret was sent to escape the Luftwaffe. A German dropped his bomb near Llanerfyl just prior to crash landing. Uncle Arthur was one of the Home Guard that arrested the young man.

* Notes found at the Omnibus archives. An essay called 'Bus operation in Mid-Wales' by K.H. Toop gives a list of the fleet as follows: Tilling Stevens 32-seaters (EM 2263 ex-Ribble and UK 6585 ex-Wolverhampton Corporation), Morris Commercial Viceroy (WJ 1411 ex-Sheffield) and a small older Ford (EV 993).

The yard of Selwyn Hughes in 1966 covered in snow. The rear of the Bedford OB, DBK 623, can be seen under the corrugated lean-to shelter. The previous owner was the Radnorshire company of Trotters of Crossgate, Llandrindod. *Gareth Evans, Llanfair Caereinion*

Note J11 SEL for 'Selwyn'. This 8-seat Mazda minibus was used for the morning and afternoon duty to Cedewain Special School at Newtown. Carol, Gareth's wife, would often be the driver. *Gareth Evans, Llanfair Caereinion*

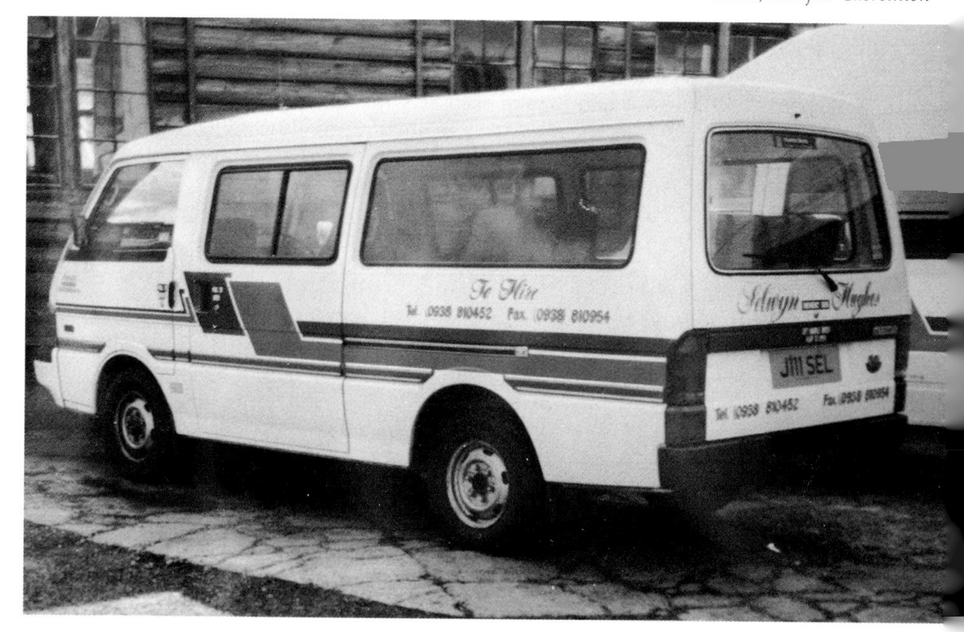

Selwyn Hughes (as recalled by Gareth Evans)

Gareth was born in the late 1940s and brought up at the Black Lion Hotel in Llanfair. Sadly, his father was to die when Gareth was very young so his mother ran the business. Selwyn Hughes had served in the Royal Navy during the war. He had rooms in the hotel and he started his business from this base. It started as a taxi business and a hospital car service. The hospital car remains an important service especially for older people in the rural areas of Powys to this day. The family would take telephone messages for Selwyn. Somewhere in the late 1950s, Selwyn expanded into school contracts and purchased a Bedford CA (Dormobile) minibus with sideways-facing bench seats.

Selwyn gathered in most of the High School contracts when MWM closed its depot and went into receivership in 1963. He purchased several second-hand coaches, the main unit was a Bedford Super Vega but he also had a Bedford OB for peak use and standby. Selwyn took on the stage route from Y Foel to Llanfair and Mondays-only to Welshpool for a short period and the main driver was John James, Bryn Gwalia (*see Chapter Fourteen*). The route was to suffer from a major problem. Passengers would be waiting on the main road for a period before the bus was due and many a passing motorist would pick the local up. The company expanded each year until the peak in the mid-1980s when there were 10 large coaches, seven midi and mini buses plus two cars for taxi duties.

The focal point of Selwyn's life was his coach company. Maybe he was a workaholic and continued to work on after most would have retired. Sadly, he was to suffer ill health and was to die soon after selling the company to Allen Watkin. Selwyn was unusual in opting to purchase new coaches instead of the normal cascading down. He had already purchased a new Bedford Duple Bella Vista 29-seater in 1965 from a cancelled Cypriot order. A new DAF LAG and a DAF Caetano were purchased in 1986.

Gareth worked for British Telecom (BT). He had a PSV licence taken on one of Selwyn's buses and would help at weekends and evenings. This would be unusual because BT always had to take priority with standby duties. Carol, the wife of Gareth, helped with the taxi and the smaller minibuses.including the Mazda.

One of the duties was the transport of special needs children and adults to Newtown. A coach left for the college of further education, plus a minibus for Cedewain School and a mini bus for Dr Richards adult centre. The coach and one minibus were parked in Newtown and the three drivers returned to Llanfair in one vehicle and would complete the return cycle in the afternoon.

Many of the accompanying photographs are from the CDT A Level project by Gareth's son. Jamie worked at the weekends for Selwyn helping to clean the coaches. The internal cleaning was done with an industrial vacuum cleaner and by hand. The outside was the use of a pressure washer, soapy water brush and a final hose down. Jamie looked at a purpose-built commercial vehicle washing machine system. The problem again shows the frugality that is needed for a small independent. A cleaning system with a capital cost of over £30,000 and an output of 25 buses/coaches per hour needs a far larger company than any that exists in Mid-Wales!

Jamie Evans (son) helped at the weekends in his final years at school. He is cleaning one of the coaches in the yard. Most Mid-Wales companies are noted for the outside and internal cleanliness of their vehicles. Other companies considered that Selwyn had the best turnout of coaches and that is no mean praise from his peers. *Gareth Evans, Llanfair Caereinion*

Demand returned for midi-buses that had been the original market dominated by the Bedford OB with 29 seats. Mercedes would have much of this market in the 1990s and this is Selwyn's example of the versatile model with 29 seats. *Gareth Evans, Llanfair Caereinion*

Every company that had long distance touring would acquire an executive vehicle. Selwyn had a Volvo B10M Plaxton. This is parked in the yard gleaming after Jamie's cleaning duty.
Gareth Evans, Llanfair Caereinion

Allen Watkins purchased the company from Selwyn Hughes. The Mercedes 707 18-seater is on the outside inspection bay. Note rear safety barrier and metal covers are in place over the pit. Such vehicles are useful for many weekend and excursion trips for smaller groups. There are not many local bookings from such a small town that require 50 plus passengers. *Author (2005)*

Part of the brickwork of the old stables of the Black Lion coaching inn can be seen on the right. The three mini-buses are LDVs. J169 HNV dating back to 1990 is an ex-British Railways crew-bus. *Author (2005)*

Allen Watkins stands beside the Leyland Van Hool. Note the logo AW using the 'A' of coach. The door of the modern steel-framed workshop hides most of the Neoplan luxury coach. This coach can be seen with Graham Sharp's Collection as brand new in Selwyn Hughes colours. It is one of the vehicles that Allen purchased on Selwyn's retirement. *Author (2005)*

Allen Watkins and Llanfair Coaches

Allen was born on a small hill farm on the upland moors behind the town at Cefn Coch in 1957. He can just remember the MWM depot at the junction for the turn to Cefn Coch on the start of the gradient to Newtown on the outskirts of the town. Selwyn Hughes took on the school contracts and excursion traffic in 1963 as recalled above. Selwyn expanded the coach yard on a site that had been the historic Black Lion coaching inn fields. Allen commenced working with Selwyn around 1980 as a part-time driver. Allen had taken on the family beef and sheep farm after the death of his father. It was easy to arrange to look after the farm and also drive the morning and afternoon school contracts. Allen is a qualified vehicle technician having served an apprenticeship with the county main Ford dealer and then with a local Llanfair garage. Gradually Allen took on more duties especially repairs and became full time in 1999. The farm is still in the family ownership but the land is let out. Allen purchased the coach business in 2003. Allen and his wife, Siân, work within a full-time partnership with Siân at base looking after all the administration.

The company has eight vehicles. There are two executives, a Scania Van Hool (ex-Shearings) and a Neoplan that Selwyn had purchased new. These are used for touring and excursion work. There are two 50-seat plus for school contract work. They are a Van Hool and a Leyland Tiger. There is a Mercedes 18-seater that Selwyn purchased new. The fleet is completed with three minibus units. All are LDVs and the oldest is a converted ex-British Railways crew bus. The current school contract is from Y Foel to Llanfair for secondary school and two routes from Rhiwhiriaeth and Lawnt for both primary and secondary children.

Allen Watkins has just checked the 53-seat Scania Van Hool so that Megan Jones can return the school children along the Upper Banwy villages to Foel at 3.50 pm. *Author (2005)*

Geraint thinks that his father started with a Crossley converted World War I fire tender ex-Royal Flying Corps. This photograph dating from the mid-1920s is almost certainly a Guy. Guy produced several small models for rural stage and excursion work before concentrating on heavy chassis municipal and provincial buses from around 1927 onwards.

Geraint Gittins, Dolanog

Geraint can just remember the 14-seat Bedford WHB when he was a child in the late 1940s. His father, Plenydd, sits on the entrance steps. It was the backbone of the World War II services and was often overcrowded. This was the first Bedford bus produced between 1931 and 1933 with bodywork by Waveney. The sales were not high but Bedford was to take off with the longer wheel based WLB with 20 seats that came on to the market in 1932. *Geraint Gittins, Dolanog*

There is frequent local hire for various societies including long distance weekend work. The extended tour business is on contract to another local business. The main section of this work is taking Americans on tours with sports themes. John Gosnall is a friend of the author and acts as courier. A recent tour was a USA ladies soccer team with visits to several grounds in the North-West such as Liverpool and also Dublin. They also played against several English, Welsh and Irish local teams. Many of the tours are golf based.

Allen and Siân have seven regular part-time staff and ladies are the backbone of the school service.

Geraint Gittins of Dolanog

Plenydd Gittins was one of a large family. His brother, Ynyr, was already trading as the owner of the village general stores. Plenydd started a garage in the early 1920s. A garage in such an isolated community needed several facets of trade to generate income for one man so a bus was purchased to add to petrol sales and car repair/servicing. The stage route would be Monday to Welshpool, Wednesday to Oswestry and also several other days to either Llanfair Caereinion or Llanfyllin for shopping. There was a charabanc. The first coach was recalled from a family story that the two brothers went to Manchester to collect a Crossley. Research indicates that Crossley produced a vehicle in volume for the Royal Flying Corps both as a staff car and a fire tender. Many were reconditioned and re-bodied as small buses for rural operators. The bus recorded in the early photographs was a Guy acquired several years later.

Geraint can remember the 14-seat Bedford and 29-seat Austin K when he was a child in the late 1940s. The Bedford had a roof rack and family tales tell that it was hopelessly overloaded during the war often with 30 people inside and the roof hanging with farm produce.

Geraint commenced an apprenticeship with Wolverhampton Motor Services. This was a division of the Rootes Group including the commercial section of Commer/Karrier. Dad was to die suddenly at the age of 59 in 1963. Geraint returned immediately to take on the business. The school bus was then the smaller section of the trade. Geraint would drive the Austin daily to Llanfair. (Both Geraint and Mair, the author's wife, would have travelled on the same bus with Plenydd driving so they could attend Llanfair High School in the late 1950s.)

Geraint operated the first privately-owned subsidized bus route in Wales in early December 1964. The stage route from Dolanog had been withdrawn 12 months previously. It was the Monday service to Welshpool and 20 of the 29 seats were vacant. The return journey cost £3 6*s*. 6*d*. The fare income was £1 16*s*. Montgomeryshire County Council and the Ministry of Transport paid the balance. The experiment did not extend over the trial period of three months. A Ministry spokesman said there remained a need to consider support for access to such isolated areas with the use of private cars, taxis or dual-purpose Post Office vehicles.

Soon Geraint started to add to the fleet and his first purchase was a Bedford with 29 seats that was nicknamed 'y dorth' or the loaf. Gradually the coach business

Above: The Bedford Duple Super Vista with 29 seats was introduced as a successor to the gap created by the 1950 withdrawal of the OB. It was based on the 4 ton forward control good chassis and sales were modest. MacBraynes in the Scottish Highlands and Islands was the volume purchaser. Geraint's version had the 300 cubic inch diesel engine. It soon acquired the nickname of 'y dorth' (the loaf). *Geraint Gittens, Dolanog*

Right: Plenydd Gittins purchased a second-hand Austin K and it was the main bus when Geraint had to return home in 1963 with the sudden death of his father. The bus is important as it operated the only trial of a subsidy for a stage route for the Ministry of Transport in rural Wales in 1964 along with three others in England and two in Scotland. Geraint is at the wheel for an article in the *The County Times* of the experiment. *Geraint Gittens, Dolanog*

Geraint has driven the DAF Van Hool to Colchester for a singing festival; Côr Meibion Dyfi (Dovey Valley Male Voice Choir) was the load. (May puns be permitted as they all paid a tenor.)
Geraint Gittens, Dolanog

The Border Mobility Co. Ford bus waits at Llanfair Caereinion ready to proceed to Y Foel. This bus supported by the community has facilities for both wheelchairs and mobile passengers. This bus connected with the Shrewsbury to Llanidloes service at Welshpool prior to leaving. Service 108a operates twice per day on Mondays to Fridays only. *Author (2005)*

RTG 749 is a Burlingham Seagull lightweight all-metal coach. Most companies ordered the Bedford chassis with a Duple body but there were options with Burlingham and Mulliner. Duple would transfer their Hendon factory into the Burlingham Blackpool unit at a later date.
The Williams family, Llangadfan

Frontal view of VCA 98. Two models of this Bedford plus a Bedford CA feeder were the basis of the service in the early 1970s. *The Williams family, Llangadfan*

increased but petrol retailing had little profit margin and ceased. Garage repairs and service would have needed extra staff and space so coaches became the sole income. The bus fleet in 2005 consisted of a Mercedes 814 D with 33 seats, a DAF Bova with 51 seats and a MAN Salvador Caetano with 35 seats. A school contract to both the primary and secondary school at Llanfair is the daily duty. Both schools book many extra day and evening trips for swimming, concerts, museum/art gallery visits and sport. Private hire especially with older groups and cultural trips for eisteddfodau and choirs is important. Tours are arranged to Scotland and Ireland according to demand. Geraint is the only full-time driver but has a valued pool of four to five drivers. The business can only succeed on the skilled purchase and maintenance of older vehicles and would never carry the depreciation cost of a new vehicle. This has been the basis of providing a bus service to the Dolanog area for a grand total of over 80 years within the skills of Plenydd and Geraint.

Geraint's stage route ceased in 1965. Crosville continued to operate a twice-daily service from Llanfair to Welshpool. This service was withdrawn leaving the town of Llanfair with no stage service except the mail bus post service. Several local councillors took up the cause. A new service started in 2002 operated by Border Mobility of Welshpool. This introduced a new concept of a bus equipped for both wheelchairs etc. and those with full mobility. The service operates twice per day from Welshpool to Y Foel. It is one of the few in the Powys timetables that lists both railway and bus connections to Shrewsbury, Birmingham etc. There is a target to try and extend the service, including that to Dinas Mawddwy and Machynlleth with support from the Powys County Council and the Welsh Assembly. Geraint Gittins has now retired.

Mrs Williams of Banwy Valley Transport

Mrs Joyce Williams was born in Doncaster and came to Dyffryn Banw as a young lady with the Land Army during World War II. Her journey for home leave was Doncaster to Welshpool by train with numerous changes, then the Crosville bus from Welshpool to Llanfair and finally on the bus of Davy John to Llangadfan. It was not unknown for the passengers to get out to push for a bump start. Thomos John Williams worked for the Montgomeryshire War Agricultural Committee and his main work was moving plant such as crawler tractors on a lorry from farm to farm. These crawler tractors were used for ploughing and reclaiming land. The pair married in 1948. Mr Williams, known locally as Thomos John, had the small Sun Garage. He started to collect children from the most isolated upland farms for Ysgol y Banw. MWM had already moved Davy John's buses to the depot at Llanfair Caereinion

The whole coach industry in the valley altered when MWM was restructured in 1962/63. Thomos John already had a Bedford CA minibus. Tudwal James and Bob Edwards had school contracts with buses to bridge the created gap. Thomos John received the school contract in 1968 and purchased the necessary coaches. Ann, the eldest of nine daughters, recalled that dad died in 1975 at the age of 50. Joyce already had a PSV licence and decided to take on the business. Ann obtained a PSV licence as soon as she was 21 to assist with evening and

The YRQ Bedford chassis with Plaxton Elite body became a very popular choice in the 1970s. This coach was purchased from Trefaldwyn Motors and sold back to them as Mrs Williams came up for retirement. *The Williams family, Llangadfan*

The last coach owned was a Volvo. Mrs Williams helps the children to return to their class at Ysgol y Banw. The coach had just returned from a visit to the swimming baths at Welshpool. *The Williams family, Llangadfan*

weekend driving so the two ladies plus several part-time drivers took up the challenge. Arwel Evans worked at the garage as the full-time mechanic. The initial coach fleet was a Bedford OB, two Bedford Vegas and two Bedford CAs as feeders. The Bedford OB was sold on to enthusiasts for restoration. The larger coaches were used for transport to the High School. An AEC was purchased from Wrexham and a Bedford YRQ Plaxton was purchased from Trefaldwyn Motors. The final coach was a Volvo. The number of children from Llanerfyl and Banw primary schools only warranted one bus for a period in the early 1990s for the journey to Llanfair High School. The Bedford was re-purchased by Trefaldwyn Motors and Joyce finished with the bus company in 1996. Selwyn Hughes purchased the Volvo and took on the school contract. Other day work was done including daytime school trips plus weekend and summer work with excursions to such places as Chester Zoo, Rhyl, Colwyn Bay and Aberystwyth. There was also a contract with a Birmingham coach company to transfer scout groups at the weekend from a summer school near Barmouth. The timing gave a load both ways. Ann recalls how mother and some of the girls cleaned the coaches every Saturday in addition to the daily tidy-up. Maldwyn Davies had a coach at Llwydiarth (*see Llanfyllin section in the next chapter*). Mrs Williams and Maldwyn would help each other when necessary. Mrs Williams, the proprietor of the Llangadfan coaches, is the widow who served the community of the valley for 20 years and they were proud of the spirit and enterprise of the lady.

Joyce is presented with a gift by Selwyn Hughes (summer 1996). The others were the drivers who worked the various school coaches from Llanfair High School: 1. Eddie Francis, 2. Allen Watkin, 3. Bob Bowden, 4. Megan Jones, 5. Arwyn Davies, 6. Martin Jones, 7. Mum or Joyce, 8. Dai Davies, 9. Heber Jones, 10. Mike the mechanic, 11. Geof Brench, 12. Selwyn Hughes, 13, Tegwyn Jones, 14. Jack Evans, 15. Geraint Gittins.

The Williams family, Llangadfan

Right: Elvin Morris stands by the company 14-seat Chevrolet LQ designed as a one-man-operated rural bus. Assembly started from USA kits at Hendon in 1923 and assembly transferred to Luton in 1929. General Motors made the decision to transfer both design and production and this led to the first Bedford bus WHB model coming off the production line in 1931.
Tanat Valley Coaches

Below: A 1947 Bedford OB Duple Vista stands at Upper Brook Street, Oswestry where many of the stage routes terminated. This vehicle (JMA 201) had the lettering of R.E. Morris. The coach was owned between 1952 and 1961.
Tanat Valley Coaches

Chapter Seven

The North-East Corner of Montgomeryshire and over the Border to England

Llanfyllin has the local High School and this generates much school contract travel. Much of the area has few people and is a further example of the 'Green Desert' of upland Central Wales. The geography can have a rough division based on the following aspects. The first is the high heather moors with sheep walks on the mass of the Berwyn Mountains with few homesteads and only one B class road that crosses to Bala. The second is that of uplands with sheep/cattle farming and forestry. Streams coming off the mountains have created deep valleys between undulating uplands of scattered farms with some small settlements, usually based around a church or chapel. The third area is that where the rivers gain volume and open up into broad fertile valleys with larger settlements. Examples are Meifod on the Afon Efyrnwy, Llanfyllin on the Afon Cain, Llansantffraid close to the confluence of the Efyrnwy and the Cain and finally Llanrhaeadr ym Mochnant in the Tanat Valley. The final area is south and east of Llanymynech as the three rivers merge and flow to the confluence of the River Severn. Parts of this almost flat land of dykes and bunds (banks or levees) would appear like the fens except for the surrounding highlands. The central flat strip of about seven miles by two miles is the sediment fill of a glacial scooped lake dating back 100,000 years. The area can suffer from flooding.

Llanfyllin became the largest settlement on the Welsh side of the border and the main market for the area. Myllin is the name of the archdeaconry, so it was important as the religious administrative area also. A railway branch line arrived here around 1865 running from Oswestry. The current A490 road is a branch also for it terminates at Llanfyllin and continues as several B roads. Through traffic is therefore limited and the town acts as a centre for travel out to other attractions. There is a large Victorian workhouse on the outskirts and this is being considered for major restoration. The town may need an attraction of such a heritage site in addition to the church, St Myllins Well, and an early non-conformist chapel, otherwise it may become little more than a dormitory town with the job losses from farm and forest mechanization. Even the town council's pamphlet only gives direction by car.

The problem or the asset is across the border. The town of Croesoswallt or Oswestry is the dominant town for trade, legal services etc. The coach companies have always traded on both sides of the border. The Cambrian Railways had its head office and workshops here and this has set a tradition of many from every part of Montgomeryshire travelling to the town. There was an enclave south of the Berwyn Massif that was in Denbighshire, but Llansilin and the surrounds have now become part of Powys.

The total area is one of a startlingly attractive and varied landscape. Lake (reservoir) Efyrnyw with the nature reserve and the waterfalls of Pistyll Rhaeadr attract many cars and some coach traffic. The isolated valley of Pennant Melangell has a gem of a medieval church on a Celtic site. There are several long distance footpaths. Some of the land has diversified into

The Llangynog-Oswestry light railway replacement service was taken over by Crosville in 1951. The Bristol SC4LK is at the top end of Willow Street in Oswestry. Tanat Valley Motors continues to operate this service. *The Omnibus Society*

Peter (*left*) and Michael (*right*) entered into partnership with their father Elvin (*centre*). The company also had the local franchise for Austin Rover at this stage in the early 1980s. *Tanat Valley Coaches*

landscaped caravan parks but this traffic is entirely dependent on cars. There are industrial relics of lead and slate at Llangynog and of limestone quarries at Llanymynech. There is a strong feeling for literature and music within the Welsh language. A Christmas postage stamp issue within a series of Christmas/New year traditions showed the Tanat Valley plygain or carols in 1986.

Llanymynech has much of transport interest. The Montgomeryshire Canal runs on the village edge and there is a long but low set aqueduct over the river. Tramways used to feed into the wharf where kilns produced burnt lime. The station was just in England on the then main Cambrian through line from Oswestry to Welshpool. The Llanfyllin line headed to the west and the Colonel Stephens' Shropshire & Montgomeryshire Light Railway line set out to Shrewsbury. Until 1925 there was a further junction off the Llanfyllin line on a spur that looped back to the Llangynog light railway (Tanat Valley branch) joining at Blodwell Junction. The line from Oswestry to Llynclys and part of the light railway will be part of a future heritage line. The main road carries much traffic including long distance coaches as it heads across Central Wales to Swansea and South-West Wales.

A salient of Wales moves into Shropshire and includes the Efyrnwy/Severn confluence and the Breidden Hills. Tanat Valley Motors runs the services from Llanymynech through Llandrinio, Crewgreen and Coedway to Shrewsbury on the northern flank; Arriva services from Llanidloes travel through Buttington, Trewern and Middletown to Shrewsbury on the southern flank. The Criggion story of the works bus to the radio station and the astonishing Criggion branch line are placed in this chapter rather than under Welshpool for literary convenience.

Tanat Valley Coaches

R.E. Morris and Sons Ltd trade as Tanat Valley Coaches. Michael and Peter, the sons, recall the history of the company centred at Llanrhaeadr-ym-mochnant. William Morgan translated 'Y Beibl' into Welsh four centuries ago when he was the priest for the parish so this parish is dear to the Welsh nation. The company serves the north-east of Montgomeryshire including the enclave of Llansilin recently transferred from Clywd and has numerous services over the border into Oswestry and Shrewsbury.

Uncle Bill was 'demobbed' in 1919 and had injuries received at Gallipoli. Hard manual rural work was not an option so he purchased a car and started to ferry people around the valley. The station was a mile from the village so this was an early taxi service. The Tanat Valley Light Railway that ran from 1904 until 1951 provided the public transport. Uncle Bill would take people and goods for the connection at Llanrhaeadr station.

Elvin Morris (father of Michael and Peter) joined his much older brother in 1925. They purchased a lorry to ferry both road stone and coal for the steamrollers as the County proceeded to metal the roads of the district. The lorry was soon used on the Wednesday of the Oswestry market to carry stock

Tanat Valley's Leyland Tiger re-bodied by Eastern Counties stops at Llansantffraid bus stop. The photograph was taken standing on the wall of the old station yard. Service 445 operates between Llanfyllin and Oswestry. *Author (2005)*

One of the most unusual coaches was the 1989 TAZ Dubrava-built in Yugoslavia. The vehicle in a white and orange livery was common in the then communist Eastern European states. Tanat Valley purchased the unit second-hand from Aron Coaches of London for Eastern European work. The officials used to think it was a local and would just wave the vehicle on. *Tanat Valley Coaches*

Bedford has an illustrious history in the supply of rural buses to the independents. The Bedford Lazer is one of several at Llanrhaeadr and would be one of the final vehicles produced before production ceased in 1984. Note the lower height of the low floor Dennis Dart with permanent indicator showing access for wheel chairs. Another Dennis Dart (R469 NEP) is the only vehicle ever purchased new with grant assistance from Powys County Council. The double-deck Leyland Olympian is one of several retained for school transport. *Author (2005)*

Double-deck Bristol VR (ex-Badger Line) and Leyland Leopard (ex-Bartons of Nottingham) both purchased for school contract work. *Tanat Valley Coaches*

Leyland National on stage route duty at Llangynog. There were few of these low entry buses available in the late 1980s. Second-hand units were available in quantity. They were not suited to long rural B routes with twists and gradients as they were an urban design. The short-lived Leyland Greenwich re-design was a great improvement. *Tanat Valley Coaches*

This Leyland Leopard is in the country lanes west of Oswestry heading toward Llanarmon Dyffryn Ceiriog. Ceiriog was the birthplace of the poet John 'Ceiriog' Hughes and Ceiriog was the manager of the Van Railway Line and lived at Caersws a century earlier. *Tanat Valley Coaches*

and people. Benches and a hood were fitted. The service expanded and a charabanc was purchased for passengers with additional use for weekend and holiday excursions. Michael is uncertain but thinks there may have been two buses by the late 1920s, including a Ford TT or AA and a Chevrolet. Service licences were obtained after 1930 and the Bedford PSV bus/coach became the standard. The company continued with both the lorry business and also a hearse. Examples of the pre-war routes now follow:

Efail-rhyd to Llansilin and over the Bwlch (pass) to Oswestry, Bwlch-y-ddar, Penybont, Llansilin and Oswestry. No licence was available for the shorter direct route to avoid duplication with the light railway. The exception was a Sunday evening service and a Saturday evening service from Oswestry. The return on Saturday at 11.00 pm from the pubs, the cinema and dances was packed and often warranted a second bus. There were two long distance summer routes to New Brighton and Colwyn Bay from the outlying villages but these were not very remunerative. The Oswestry market buses would have a roof rack fixed for the day to carry goods in and purchases back. The emergency door was at the rear. This would open and a calf in a hessian sack would then be placed under the rear seat so up to four calves could be carried back to the valley. There are numerous anecdotes of rural mishaps. An older man caused concern to a very prim chapel lady. He was happy with beer. The calf and the sack slid forward under the seat and the calf licked the ankle of the lady. She thought the old boy was getting amorous and hit him with her shopping bag!

Business was maintained during World War II. This would have seen the final flourish of the competing light railway helped by use of indigenous coal. The prisoner of war camp at Llanrhaeadr generated extra business. The Italians were delivered to the farms in the morning and collected in the evening. There was a Saturday service for them to Oswestry with a late return. A guard with a rifle was on the bus but he never had any use for the weapon. Dad was very fond of choral singing and he would request that the Italians sing to him when he was driving the bus back home. Several Italians made a model boat for the older brother of Peter and Michael.

The bus service expanded after the war as people started to work away from the family farms. The 1944 Education Act both raised the school leaving age and phased out the all-age village schools. The light railway closed in 1951 and Crosville took on the service. The Llanfyllin branch closed in 1965 and Parish took on that duty (*see below*). Both services transferred to Tanat Valley after deregulation (Crosville) and retirement (Parish). The original garage of the 1920s was an ex-Liverpool Corporation shed (Vrynwy reservoir pipeline maintenance) but this became too small so the current site was purchased around 1980.

Uncle Bill had retired in the early 1950s and Elvin carried on until the two boys could join. Peter came in after his apprenticeship in 1975 and Michael joined in 1977. Tanat Valley Coaches is the currently largest bus company in Montgomeryshire. The company has 40 PSV vehicles, 35 full-time staff are employed and there is a further pool of over 25 part-time drivers. Nick Culliford is the senior clerical officer and was an ex-staff member of the Oswestry Crosville depot. Michael estimates that 60 per cent of the business is

Two Metro-Cammell Weymanns with Cummins L10 diesel engines were purchased for Continental School Tours with a contract in the Birmingham area. These Metroliners were ex-Crosville/ National Express. The double-decker has now been relegated to school duties. The single-decker is a Leyland Leopard (ex-Kinch of Nottingham). It has Bus Clywd in the window. Clwyd County Council ceased in 1996 and was broken up into Flint, Denbighshire and Wrexham Maelor. The section of Glyndŵr of Moelfre, Llangedwyn and Llansilin became part of Powys.

Tanat Valley Coaches

Tanat Valley Coaches Mercedes left Llanfyllin at 8.45 to arrive in Welshpool at 9.23 am. It waits until 10.00 before proceeding to Churchstoke. This is the main bus stop for the town and is situated away from the shops where the street widens and where up to 20 buses call on each side of the street.

Author (2005)

school contract work especially to Llanfyllin High School and the Marchers School at Oswestry. A further 20 per cent is stage routes. Some are fully commercial and others receive support from either Bws Powys or Shropshire Bus. The services include Oswestry town service, Ellesmere to Oswestry (another ex-rail route), Llangynog to Oswestry, Llanfyllin to Oswestry, Llanfyllin to Welshpool via Meifod, Welshpool to Churchstoke via Montgomery and college term time only of Llanrhaeadr to Newtown. Four Crosses to Shrewsbury was a route operated by MWM in the 1940s and 1950s and included a diversion into Criggion while the current service moves directly on the B road from Llandrinio to Crew Green. This route during the MWM reign also included extras for the days of the Loton Park hill climb. (This motor sport with cars such as Dellow is now history.) The Shrawardine Oswestry Wednesday-only service was withdrawn in 2004 once Shropshire Bus withdrew financial support; this was the last vestige of Gittins bus service. A Llanwyddyn via Llanfyllin and Llanymynech service operates to Shrewsbury on the first Saturday of the month and to Wrexham on the third Saturday. Express stage routes operate in the summer. These are to Blackpool every Saturday, Aberystwyth every Friday and Llandudno via Bala over the Berwyn every Monday. Excursions, leisure and long distance tours account for the remaining 20 per cent of the business. The company pioneered Eastern Europe tours and must have had the first Welsh coach ever to go on the ferry from Gdansk to Helsinki. One six-day tour in 2005 could only come from either Mid-Wales or the Cheviot Borders. It was to the World Sheep Dogs trials at Tullamore in the Republic of Ireland.

The fleet was still operating the last of the Bedford coaches, then 20 years plus since manufacture. It still retains seven double-decks for school contracts but these will gradually be withdrawn. (See Chapter Four for the solution with 3 by 2 seat single-deckers with 70-seat capacity.) There are three low-floor Dennis units for disabled and elderly access. This includes the only new bus ever purchased with Bws Powys support. There are two long distance executives for the tour trade. The remaining fleet contains minibuses, midi-buses and second-hand single-deck coaches and buses. The two brothers not only provide a transport service but also provide much employment in the upland valley of North Montgomeryshire.

The Llanfihangel Coach Company

Both Kathleen Davies of Llywidiarth (daughter of Idris) and Margaret Jones of Llanfyllin (daughter of Maldwyn) helped to recollect the story of their grandfather and his bus company at the home of Charlotte, the widow of Maldwyn. Tom started in transport with a pony and trap son after leaving the army in 1919. The business also had a small shop. A Ford (EP 786) was purchased around 1922 and soon added both livestock and passenger delivery to Llanfyllin with adaptation of the lorry body. A Chevrolet bus was acquired in the late 1920s. Stage routes were licensed with the Traffic Commissioners from 1930 onwards and continued until coach dispersal in 1980. A Bedford

The party from Llanfihangel-yng-Gwynfa prepare to return home from the Powys Eisteddfod at Llanfair Caereinion in 1913. Everyone is in their Sunday best including the horses. Note the astounding change to 1934 when Davies arranged to take a party to Southport in his Chevrolet.

Copyright LWF0292, Dr W.T.R. Pryce, Cardiff

Tom Davies stands in the entrance of his Chevrolet on a Sunday school trip to Southport in 1934. The bus service from Llanfihangel-yng-ngwynfa provided an entry for an isolated community into a fuller life in the 1920s. A journey to Southport would have been an incredible adventure.

Kathleen Davies, Llwydiarth

WLB served during the overloaded period of World War II. A taxi was also part of the service. An austerity OWB followed in the late 1940s and the company then had two Bedford Duple OBs (including MFM 39, 'Bus to Bosworth'). The final Bedford, CUJ 261, was used in the 1970s until Maldwyn retired in 1980. Idris opted to start his own garage/shop/taxi service at Llywidiarth. Sadly Tom died in 1969 in a traffic-related accident and was still working with his sons. Morris of Llanfyllin took on the business. Both ladies have retained some records and some photographs and several examples are included.

An invoice was issued from Coopers of Prestatyn for the purchased of a second-hand Bedford OB Duple for £1444 on 28th September, 1953.

Examples of excursion hire for use of 29-seat bus:

10th July, 1965. Liverpool Corporation Estate. Llanwddyn to Trawsfynydd @ £9 8*s*. 8*d*.
4th August 1965. Churchwardens of Llanwddyn to Rhyl @ £13
25th June, 1966. Secretary Sardis Chapel to Southport @ £33 2*s*. 6*d*.
28th May, 1968. Headmaster, Llanfihangel School to Chester Zoo @ £9 3*s*. 4*d*.
6th July, 1968. Secretary Sardis Chapel to New Brighton @ £14

Examples of fare income for August 1969 when car use had a major impact on trading.

Welshpool		*Oswestry*	
4th	£4 0*s*. 0*d*.	6th	£8 12*s* 0*d*.
11th	£3 8*s*. 0*d*.	13th	£11 8*s*. 0*d*.
18th	£2 17*s*. 6*d*.	20th	£12 12*s*. 0*d*.
15th	£5 11*s*. 0*d*.	27th	£11 7*s*. 0*d*.

Stage routes

Llanwddyn to Welshpool every Monday, to Oswestry every Wednesday, to Llanfyllin every Thursday and to Oswestry every Saturday.

The service was valued over a period of 60 years with a peak demand from 1940 until 1955. Such a family company always had to run within a strict budget, with skilled use of second-hand coaches and maintenance carried out within their own workshop. Companies helped each other with vehicles and drivers. Tom both gave and received help from Parish of Morda.

A service operated in 2005 on Wednesdays and Fridays with a Community Bus hired by the parish to Llanfyllin with connections for Oswestry. A Dial-a-Ride service could be pre-booked on Mondays, Tuesdays and Thursdays. Tanat Valley Motors have a journey to Shrewsbury (first Saturday of each month) and Wrexham (third Saturday of each month) that commences at Llanwddyn. The village of Llanwddyn receives many visitors by car and private coach hire as the new village is at the foot of the dam of Lake Vyrnwy with many scenic attractions.

Alwyn Rees was to publish a minor classic of social history and this research was published in 1940 entitled *Life in the Welsh Countryside*. This was based on the parish of Llanfihangel-yng-Ngwynfa where he describes the social structure of the 1930s before electricity, radio, TV and the mobility of the car would alter this isolated upland parish in the shadow of the Berwyn Mountains. The following contains a précis from within the book held in Newtown library:

Kathleen's father, Idris (*left*) and Maldwyn (*right*) stand in front of their Bedford OB Duple. *Kathleen Davies, Llwydiarth*

World War II taxi fitted with wartime headlight cowls. Make uncertain but maybe an Armstrong Siddeley.

Margaret Jones, Llanfyllin

The late 1940s' Bedford WLB UJ 4806 had worked hard during World War II. The service warranted a second Bedford Standard Austerity OWB DCA 181 (*left*).

Margaret Jones, Llanfyllin

Two Bedford OB Duples worked through the 1960s and were sold to Mid-Wales Motorways. MFM 39 started with Crosville in 1950 and was to become the 'Bus to Bosworth' (*see Chapter Ten*). *Margaret Jones, Llanfyllin*

GDM 644 (ex-Davies), destination Kerry & Sarn, is parked with another OB at the far end of the Gravel Park at Newtown on the edge of the Severn bank. The flood prevention construction has realigned the river and the background is now a car park. *Margaret Jones, Llanfyllin*

Bedford MUN 92 replaced the two OBs in the early 1970s. It could be an example of an earlier SB chassis Bedford dating from the late 1950s. It is shown parked at Oswestry.

Margaret Jones, Llanfyllin

Maldwyn Davies (Margaret's father) stands in front of the final Bedford (CUJ 261C) owned in the last years of operation in the late 1970s. Maybe the sheep dog was needed to find passengers in this very isolated upland area?

Margaret Jones, Llanfyllin

One of the shopkeepers in Llan is also the bus and hackney carriage proprietor. The bus has given an improved facility to make the market town of Oswestry more accessible. Both stock transport and shopping is now done and has brought the area into an increased cash economy with less barter. Clothes, furniture and household goods are now purchased in either Llanfyllin or Oswestry with an occasional trip as far as Liverpool. The Oswestry mart is the main attraction. The cinema at Oswestry attracts a few young Welsh speakers but otherwise has little to offer this traditional community so it does not pay to run a stage bus except on market day. A competition in an eisteddfod generates more interest than football or horse racing. A full coach would go to such a cultural event. The spring and autumn fairs at Llanfair and Llanfyllin are popular. Llanerfyl still held a 'gwylmabsant'. This annual event was known as Ffair Ffyliad (fools fair) and was held on the first Tuesday of May. It was a leisure event with an origin of baiting, wrestling and interludes (short dramas). The gathering started at 3.00 pm to peak around 10.00 pm and disperse at 3.00 am. The buses from the local hamlets were packed to overflow on this day. [There is no mention of the car.]

The community researched and updated this work in 2004. The volume is entitled *A Welsh Countryside Revisited*. It looks back on the closure of many village schools and shops and the use of a mobile shop-van for a period in the 1950/60s. The car dominates transport: the car is now used for a weekly shop to either Welshpool or Oswestry with 11 per cent travelling to Shrewsbury. Fashion shopping (a concept unknown in 1930) will be done in Shrewsbury or Chester. The access to the motorcar has revolutionized the young women's role freeing them from the ties of the house and the farmyard. Many make a valuable contribution to the community by salaries earned in the surrounding towns. [The rural bus is no longer worthy of mention. This ignores the vital duty of school contracts as if the bus is invisible.]

Evans had the garage at the Llanfihangel turn and also had taxis and school collection. He held the Chevrolet at the back of his yard for a number of years until it was a rotted shell.

Llanfyllin High School and school transport history

The High Schools (grammar schools) of Montgomeryshire came into existence in the 1890s as the various 1870s Education Acts gained strength. They were for scholarship and fee-paying children. The majority of children stayed at what was to become 'all-age schools'. The high schools were very small units even into the 1930s. The local children both from the town and surrounding villages walked daily. The schools had to provide lodgings for the children from the furthest hamlets and farms. Llanfyllin was typical of the six schools where children could face a daunting task of attendance. Some walked six miles while others came in with the local carrier. There were many daily horse-drawn carrier routes to the railhead. Some had to walk several miles to the pick-up point for the carrier. The journey could take up to two hours plus and was a cold, wet experience. The Monday and Friday travel was such a problem that many yeomen with a little more wealth sent their children to a minor public school. Provision gradually increased in the inter-war years. The bicycle often became the reward for passing the scholarship and also solved the means of

T.R. Morris operated around 10 coaches and minibuses at the peak activity in the 1990s. All coaches were Bedfords and the minibus shown is a Ford Transit. The photograph was taken in the yard at Llanfyllin. The wooden-framed corrugated-iron shed protected on the outside with bitumen paint is typical of many vehicle shelters in rural Wales. *Graham Sharp, Newtown*

A Dennis with Spicer body for 20 seats was the mainstay in the early 1930s. Note the wider entry door with low running board for easy entrance. This was a feature of the small Dennis bus in the late 1920s. *Ivor Parish*

getting to school. It is recalled that, by 1940, the headmaster declared, 'the place resembles a scrap iron heap' and an attempt was made to arrange bike parking.

The local bus company for Llanfyllin commenced in 1920 and was owned by Tom Morris. He commenced with a Model T Ford with a Wednesday service to Oswestry market and a Thursday service into Llanfyllin from the local villages. The bus changed for a 14-seat Chevrolet in 1930 and a 20-seat Bedford was acquired in 1934. A school bus with the Chevrolet started from Brithdir around 1931. The railway branch line carried children and the service of the 1920s shows departure from Llansantffraid at 8.44 am, Llanfechain at 8.49, a request stop at Bryngwyn and arrival at Llanfyllin at 9.05 am. There was a departure from Llanfyllin at 4.30 pm. (Pupils also used the trains until 1965 to Machynlleth, Llanidloes, Newtown, Welshpool and Oswestry.) Far more children started to attend after the Education Act of 1944. Llanrhaeadr Secondary Modern closed so that Llanfyllin became the sole secondary school for a very large catchment area of few people. Route extension took place and Morris's fleet increased until the company peaked with 12 vehicles. Stage routes and excursion traffic was also important. The family company continued with Tom's children. John and Margaret have recently retired and the bulk of delivery to Llanfyllin is now within Tanat Valley Motors portfolio.

(This essay is sourced from the centenary book, *Llanfyllin High School 1897 to 1997*, edited by Pauline Page-Jones from a copy held by Melfyn Jones at Newtown.)

Ivor Parish and the Morda bus/coach company

Ivor's father served in both the Army and the newly formed RAF during World War I. He served in Palestine as the Ottoman Empire broke up and he was within the short-lived technology of the Balloon Regiment. He trained at the Park Hall Army camp near Oswestry and met mother who worked in the corner shop at Morda. They married after the war and moved to grandfather's home for a short while at Barry in South Wales. They returned to Morda and father started light haulage work with a Ford T flat lorry to carry coal and sundries. He built a light bus frame that was held on a gantry and this was bolted to the flat every Wednesday and Saturday to work into Oswestry from the Llanyblodwel area. Demand was such that the bus business soon dominated turnover. A Harry Evans operated from Llansantffraid and the route plus bus was purchased around 1926. This service was extended to Llanfechain and was the basis of the rail replacement service nearly 40 years later. The company now had five vehicles.

The business expanded after World War II with both the school contracts and the brief boom before the dominance of the private car. Much of the contract work was over the border from Morda with Montgomeryshire LEA. The first was a taxi run for the isolated farms and houses that fed Trefnannau Primary School. This was Ivor's first duty after he returned from National Service as he was still several months too young for a PSV licence. The successor-company still has this contract. The company soon had two buses to the then Welshpool

The school taxi (often a pre-war big 'Yank') became a feature for rural school in the late 1940s. Previously children walked over three miles and sometimes the punishment books show a reprimand for being late. Minibus units such as the Bedford CA, the Standard Atlas and BMC versions badged as either Austin or Morris soon replaced the taxis. The 1938 Packard was used for Trefnannau school and would accommodate up to seven children. *Ivor Parish*

The early 1930s Bedford WLB with 20 seats was the winner that started to take Bedford to the light market dominance. This example had a Thurgood body. *Ivor Parish*

The 1938 Bedford Duple with 26 seats seen after an accident with a horse that hit the bus in a panic near Trefnannau. The bus limped back to depot with one extra horsepower. *Ivor Parish*

The 1938 AEC Regal came on to site with a six-cylinder petrol engine but was converted to diesel in the 1950s. The only other half-cab owned was a Crossley. *Ivor Parish*

The 1955 Bedford Super Vega arrived in the yard in Southern Vectis livery (Isle of Wight). The petrol engine had already been changed for a Perkins diesel. *Ivor Parish*

A line of Bedfords with three different bodies parked in the Morda yard in the early 1970s. The nearest is a Duple, a Yeates petrol vehicle is in the centre and the final unit is a Burlingham with a diesel engine. *Ivor Parish*

Secondary and Grammar School. The first was via Deuddwr and Pentrebeirdd and the second dovetailed in with the Criggion works bus.

Two buses left Oswestry every weekday at 7.25 am for Criggion Radio Station. The first was known as the day workers and worked to Criggion to arrive at 8.00 am. It then immediately worked back via Criggion village, Coedway, Crewgreen and Llandrinio with the Welshpool secondary children to Four Crosses station where they transferred to the train. The reverse took place collecting the children around 4.15 pm and to collect the workers at Criggion at 5.00 pm. The bus was left for the day at Four Crosses station, the Trefnannau taxi collecting both the drivers from Welshpool and Four Crosses unless a bus was needed for mid-day work. The second bus deployed was known as 'the technicians'. It arrived at Criggion at 8.00 am to unload the day shift and immediately returned with the night shift. The bus left Oswestry again at 3.25 to take the shift change at 4.00 pm. The third bus left Oswestry at 10.25 for shift change at 11.00 pm. The weekend shifts were two by 12 hours at 8.00 am and 8.00 pm. The works bus started in 1942 with Hampsons but switched to Parish from 1950 to 1965 when it reverted to Hampsons for a few years until private car use caused withdrawal. The route started with Commer Q4 (side valve petrol engine) and the Bedford OBs.

The work bus duty was revoked at the request of Parish in 1965 for an amazing event for a small independent. The closure of the Cambrian line between Whitchurch and Buttington Junction took place including the Llanfyllin branch. Crosville received the contract for Oswestry to Welshpool but Parish was to work the Llanfyllin to Oswestry rail replacement service with a common ticket arrangement for the joint route from Llanymynech. The route had a guarantee for a certain period, maybe four years.

The company absorbed two other locals as they retired. They were Tom France of Llanymynech and Dan & Jack Gittins of Crickheath. The company must have peaked at 15 vehicles around 1970. A works bus worked to the Laura Ashley unit at Oswestry in the late 1970s. Laura Ashley Fabrics and Furniture Fittings expanded rapidly and peaked in the 1980s with factories at Caernarfon, Wrexham, Oswestry, Newtown and Carno until fierce competition forced them to move manufacture to Asia. Most vehicles were either Commers or Bedfords but there was also an AEC and a Crossley half-cab in the early 1950s. The fleet was mainly Bedfords by the 1980s. Two Commers had the two-stroke TS3 horizontally-opposed diesel engines. These were very economic on fuel but would send out a puff of smoke as they drew away from the bus stop after idling.

Father died in 1964 and the two sons, Roger and Ivor, ran the company as a partnership. Roger was 11 years older than Ivor so it was decided to sell the bulk of the business in 1982 and to continue with four minibuses only with the contracts for disabled children for both Shropshire and Powys Social Services. The bus section in 1982 was sold to Fred Owen who started to concentrate on touring to create Owens of Oswestry that now incorporates Stratos of Newtown. Sadly Roger had a stroke in 1999 so Ifor opted to retire in 2001 and sold the minibus company to Tinsleys of Maesbury who decided to continue under the brand name of Parish. Ivor was invited out one day and he was presented with a diecast model Bedford Vega that was painted in black and

The Commer Q4 with Santos body had a side valve engine. The vehicle was rugged and simple. It was a good country bus but had one fault of heavy petrol consumption. It was often used as the Criggion works bus in the early 1950s. *Ivor Parish*

Plaxton produced a forward control conversion on Bedford OBs. The driving position was moved forward but the gear lever was not altered so the driver had to reach backwards. The re-design gained *one* extra seat. The interior was pure art deco. Plaxton was one of a number of small bodywork companies in the late 1940s but was poised to expand. *Ivor Parish*

Danny and John Gittins worked from Crickheath (just east of Llanymynech) to Oswestry with stage routes that meandered along the side lanes. The Bedford OB was kept in immaculate condition and was housed overnight in a garage with radiators and draught sealing surrounding the doors. Danny was the driver with a mop of blonde hair and John was the conductor with unknown hairstyle, as he never removed his flat cap. *David Hughes, Shrewsbury*

An Albion Nimbus owned by Hampsons of Oswestry parked at Llandudno on excursion traffic. The Nimbus was used for the Oswestry Town service and also to carry staff on the works bus to Criggion Radio Station after 1965 when Parish took on the Llanfyllin branch line replacement service. *David Pye, Worthen and The Omnibus Society*

David Owen progressed from a cycle shop (1890s) to a garage with a taxi service prior to World War I. David purchased a Model T Ford bus in 1921 for local excursion and stage work.

Meifod Local History Group

The bus was sold on to Jones of Pentrebeirdd near Guilsfield. The bus lasted for 20 years plus. It has been restored and is in the local ownership of P.E. Watson-Smyth and is on loan to the Beaulieu Motor Museum. The photograph was taken at the annual Welshpool Festival of Transport. A further note by K.H. Toop was found in a 1939 Omnibus Society article. The owner, Mr Jones, had a wooden leg so the Model T had a special adaptation so Mr Jones could drive the vehicle.

Graham Sharp, Newtown

orange livery with 'Parish' on the side. The other historic Oswestry area companies were Hampsons, Vaggs of Knockin Heath, Bartleys of Selattyn, Gittins and France. Salopia of Whitchurch also had much business in the area. Much of the local transport work was with the origin of the Cambrian Railways which had its head office at Oswestry so there has always been much cross-border business. Morda is a little enclave south and west of Oswestry where all the villages such as Trefonnen, Nantmawr and Llanyblodwel, plus most farm names, still retain their Welsh origin. There is a well-preserved turnpike gate cottage on the border. This village is a mouthful with the full name of Pen-y-bont Llanerch Emrys. Political borders are never a tidy arrangement. The rivers, the birds and the bus companies ignore such borders.

Roger became secretary at one stage of the Montgomeryshire Bus and Coach Association to guide pricing with school contracts.

Gwyn Jones of Meifod

Many parishes of rural Montgomeryshire are very scattered and with few people. The rail services including light rail had arrived in larger villages by World War I with several exceptions. Examples of the larger communities must have been Churchstoke, Berriew and Meifod. These villages were large enough to have a range of services such as various shops, tailors, cobbler, school with five-plus teachers, doctor, smithy etc. The Owen family graduated from general smiths to add a cycle shop and then a garage for cars and motorcycles. This was established before World War I. David Owen was to purchase a Model T Ford bus in 1921. Bert Griffiths took on the company in the 1940s and continued with a bus for school transport.

Gwyn Jones took on the garage in 1972. Gwyn was a Tanat Valley lad and would have travelled on buses driven by Elvin Morris to school. The family moved to Oswestry so Gwyn received his final secondary education over the border. He became an apprentice for an agricultural engineer and learnt his engine/transmission skills on Nuffield and David Brown tractors. He advanced within this multi-branch company and they moved him to Cheshire as a salesman. Gwyn with his wife Jean just longed to return to Northern Montgomeryshire, so he took the risk and opportunity to purchase the Meifod garage when Bert Griffiths wanted to retire. He therefore inherited the light bus with duties to bring children in from the outlying area to Meifod Primary School. He ceased petrol sales several decades ago but continues a car repair and MOT service

The older children attended Llanfair School and Dennis Gwalchmai had the contract with a large coach. Then Dennis wished to retire so Gwyn purchased his Bedford Super Vega and the goodwill that included weekend, evening and holiday trips. The coach section was soon to be the dominant section of the trade. It truly is a family business. Both Martin, the son, and Jean have PSV licences. Several friends also help out at peak periods. The business has education contracts to Coleg Powys in Newtown, to Llanfair High School and to collect the local primary school children.

Gwyn's first purchase was in 1975 when the bus business was still based on the collection of primary school children. The Ford Transit is four to five years older than indicated by the plates, as it was an ex-military hospital bus on military plates. *Gwyn Jones, Meifod*

Gwyn purchased Dennis Gwalchmai's buses and contracts when Dennis opted to retire. One of the first larger coaches purchased came from Robinsons of Appleby in Cumbria. The DAF Plaxton Supreme was still in original livery awaiting respray. It was stationed at Meifod from 1986 until 1999. *Gwyn Jones, Meifod*

The Mercedes is the current coach for touring etc. It is seen at the coach park of Moffet Woollen Mills in Scotland. Gwyn here takes the opportunity to clean the bodywork of the grime that builds up on any long journey. *Gwyn Jones, Meifod*

The garage at Meifod shows the coaches parked on what was the petrol forecourt. The previous owner, Bert Griffiths, demolished the old buildings and replaced it with the current structure between 1948 and 1951. The total fleet is seen: there are two Caetano midi-coaches with one used daily for transport of students to Coleg Powys (Further Education College), a DAF Plaxton for secondary school contract and finally the Mercedes 0303 for excursion and tour work. *Author (2005)*

Criggion radio station works buses left Oswestry via Pant, Llanymynech and Four Crosses to cross the bridge at Llandrinio and then turn left down the accommodation lane to Criggion. Staffing was essential by technicians during the 24 hours for every day of the week. The Severn can flood across the flood plain so the coach could then only get as far at the bridge at Llandrinio. The station DUKW drives through the flood using wheel transmission bringing staff for shift change. The vehicle nicknamed 'duck' stands for USA military serial numbers. This is based on D for model year, U for amphibian, K for all-wheel drive and W for dual rear axle.

Ivor Parish

One coach worked the three technician shifts but a second coach was needed for the day maintenance staff. A Bedford OB (*above left*) would often be on duty and would then proceed to collect Welshpool Secondary children to place them on the train at Four Crosses. The DUKW (*above right*) can be seen crossing the Severn to the dry Llandrinio side to meet the coach. This must be one of the most unusual examples of 'all change please'. *(Both) Ivor Parish*

There is work such as taking children to the swimming pool at Welshpool and other sports or cultural events during the day. Gwyn maintains a luxury coach (currently a Mercedes 0303) for school contract, weekend work and holiday tours. Gwyn had also absorbed some of the work of Les Hughes in the early 1980s. Les had one old bus in the Pontrobert area. Mike Lewis does the secondary run from Pontrobert. Tanat Valley Coaches works the daily stage route between Llanfyllin and Welshpool. Meifod could easily be placed in the Llanfair or Welshpool chapters as the village easily connects with any of the three towns.

Transport at Criggion

Criggion is an isolated community on the eastern bank of the River Severn at the foot of the Breidden Hills. A branch line was built and this included several stations. The main traffic was the stone from the then Breidden Quarry Co. The stone is of very high quality for road surfacing and several major bypasses of the 1930s for towns came from this source. It is still quarried within the Hansons Company with road traffic entry and exit on one road only. Col Stephens attempted to increase traffic with camping and facilities for boats at Criggion. Criggion remains a car tourist attraction. There is a car park at the foot of the hill. The foot climb is to Rodney's Pillar and gives an excellent view.

The General Post Office and later British Telecom owned the radio station at Criggion from 1942 to 2003. It was built to support Crick near Rugby is case of destruction by enemy action. Much of the work was with maritime monitoring, working latterly for the Royal Navy, NATO and the USA. It became technically obsolete due to satellite development and a reduction of need with the conclusion of 'the cold war' with no need to monitor USSR submarine movements. The final low frequency masts were demolished in 2003.

Stan Brown, a retired engineer recalls the following. Some of the heavy equipment during the war came in on the branch line as the whole Potts system had a final boost with the War Department weapon storage systems. The extremely rural area needed works buses. These came from Oswestry. Contracts were with either Parish or Hampsons over the years. Over 200 staff were employed at the peak around 1948. The works buses delivered both day staff for maintenance etc. and the technicians that had to staff the system, in continuous use. A number of local men also cycled in from Trewern, Crewgreen etc. A DUKW was held on site as the areas between the masts were subject to flooding. The exchange between bus and DUKW is illustrated within the photography from Ivor Parish. Stan was a key engineer and would sometimes use the works bus but he also had the authority including petrol and a private car for any emergency use or extended hours during the 1940s. Car use became more frequent so only one bus was in use by the late 1960s and finally all staff came on to site in their own vehicles. A sense of dereliction with weeds starting to encroach on the site greets a traveller on the narrow lanes between Trewern and Llandrinio. There is now no stage route service to Criggion and the nearest service is the Tanat Valley bus between Llanymynech and Shrewsbury. Villagers can use the school bus to Llanfyllin during term time only.

Traces of transport past may be seen in every town. The canal boat has special extras so that wheel chairs can be accommodated. It is entering the narrow aqueduct over the Lledan brook and has just passed under the bridge that carried the Llanfair Railway a few yards after leaving the exchange sidings at Welshpool.
Author (2005)

Mike Cookson's grandfather was a brother to the Cooksons that founded the Newtown bus company around 1919. The family photograph shows the Cookson charabanc with a full load in the mid-1920s.
Mike Cookson

Chapter Eight

Welshpool and the Surrounding Area

If Oswestry is promoted as the town on the edge, Welshpool must be the Welsh border town. If it had been sited in Spain, it would be called Welshpool de la frontera. Historically the town competed with Montgomery during Norman times but it has been the larger of the two towns for centuries. It has many Georgian brick buildings in the centre. It is thought the Welsh prefix was added to Pool to avoid any confusion with other Pools, such as Poole in Dorset as both had late-medieval importance. The Welsh name is Trallwng, that again means pool. The river meanders and creates ox-bow lakes. These have the local name of 'flash' and one is a local nature reserve.

The town has a major tourist attraction of Powis Castle and Gardens. The transport history is continuous over the centuries. Poolquay was the furthest point upstream to sail and drag the Severn trows (flat bottom boats). There is still evidence of turnpikes and coaching inns. The renovated canal is an attractive feature in the centre of the town. Both standard gauge through lines and a narrow gauge light railway made the town important for railways. The trunk roads through the centre of the town became subject to chronic delays and a bypass was finally built in the early 1990s on the former railway line. This caused both the station and the line to be re-aligned leaving the old station isolated. This station was the head office for the Newtown and Oswestry Railway. The large building is now a retail complex specializing in wool products and attracts both cars and coaches in some volume. The livestock market is very large and used to attract a wide range of Monday-only bus services. There are few now as every farmer has access to several vehicles. Newtown still attracts many Tuesday-only services but their market is a street fair for the general public.

Welshpool has a wide range of shops and several supermarkets that attract car and stage route customers throughout the week. It is a vibrant small town with good public transport access. There has been pressure, including the recent past, for an off-road bus station. The main bus stop is at the upper end of the town where the High Street widens and it does face some challenge for an older person with shopping bags. The cars have the best central parking facilities. All services at Newtown, Machynlleth and Llanidloes have very central pick-up points but Welshpool has certain services such as National Express that call at the Tourist Office away from the main bus stop. The Crosville services to Llanfair and Oswestry originated as rail replacements and used to depart from the station but connections to the railway station are now poor. The Powysland Museum has a major exhibit on the canals and is housed in a canal wharf warehouse. A Festival of Transport is held every summer and will attract several vintage buses. The Llanfair Railway now has been extended to Raven Square on the outskirts of the town but it would be difficult to see that the total route through the narrow streets of the town could be extended to the standard gauge station.

One of several Ford Transits used for school feeder services. This was purchased from Boultons of Shropshire. *Author (2005)*

The expanding business now has several executive vehicles such as this Volvo with Van Hool body parked in the yard at Hope Lane, Welshpool. *Author (2005)*

Montgomery is the smaller town. It has the attraction of Montgomery Castle. Cadw (Welsh Heritage) owns both Montgomery and Dolforwyn Castle near Abermule. Access is not easy to either for a coach or for older people with decreasing mobility. After all, both were built as defence castles. Montgomery station is two miles from the town and various plans to connect the town to rail never came to fruition. The trunk road from Newtown to Craven Arms runs several miles south of the town. All this is now a heritage advantage as buildings from the Elizabethan to Georgian still stand. The town has an adequate stage service during the day with am/pm service to Newtown (Crossgate Motors), three daytime services to Welshpool and Churchstoke (Tanat Valley Motors) and three to four daily services to Shrewsbury (Worthen Motors). Skill with timetable reading will identify several market day-only services that wander along the byways. There was a coach company called Trefaldwyn Motors that traded until the owner retired a few years ago. (Trefaldwyn is the Welsh word for Montgomery.)

The total area around Welshpool contains some of the best farming land in the county and this conveys a greater sense of prosperity over the decades. The area contains some stark uplands and the combination gives a highly valued scenic landscape. Much of the border area can be walked as part of the long distance Offa's Dyke and Severn Way. One path is the start or the end of the Glyndŵr Way.

The Welshpool Companies

The town was well served by railways. Mid-Wales Motorways and Crosville dominated the stage routes. MWM maintained a depot in the town (ex-Tudors) and Crosville parked buses overnight that were based at the Oswestry depot. Arriva Midlands North operates the current main stage routes from Llanidloes to Shrewsbury and Welshpool to Oswestry. A pattern of small independents for school contracts etc. has existed for many years especially in the surrounding villages. The name of John Cookson of Newtown is important in local bus industry, as Cookson was one of the companies within the MWM co-operative founded in 1937. The story now completes a circle.

Mike Cookson started a coach company in March 2002 diversifying from an agricultural engineering base. John Cookson was one of four brothers. Mike's grandfather was one of the brothers but great uncle John had died long before Mike came on the scene. Mike wonders if there is a gene within the family with a mechanical trait. Another branch of this extended family was R.E. Cookson of Dyffryn, Berriew. Their lorries hauled coal from South Wales until the industry declined in the mid-1980s.

Mike started in March 2002 with a Ford Transit and tendered for school contracts. He speculated and purchased a full executive Volvo Van Hool for private hire in June of the same year. Two older Leyland Leopards followed immediately for two secondary school contracts. The business ran parallel with the agricultural engineering repairs. A further Van Hool was purchased in 2003. Further school contracts followed in 2004 and the agricultural machine repair

The agricultural engineering workshop was built in 1974. The business has virtually completed the switch to coach travel. The midi Caetano is over the pit and a Van Hool outline in the shed is being resprayed in Cookson's livery. A coach/lorry factor van has called with spare parts. *Author (2005)*

School contract work requires an older bus as winter duties may only be several hours each day. The Leyland Leopard is ex-Liverpool City Coaches. Leylands will gradually become as rare as operating Bedfords over the next few years. *Author (2005)*

started to be reduced. Many school contracts had been with Crosville. Arriva opted to concentrate on stage routes. The company had to maintain permanent staff and local independents can often offer school contracts plus flexibility of local excursions at a lower price and yet maintain viability.

Mike discussed the business at his premises at Hope Lane in late-April, 2005. The fleet was then six Van Hools of 50 seats on Volvo, DAF and Leyland chassis, three midi units (21 to 35 seats) and three minibuses. Both Mike and his wife, Chris, work full time with Chris helping with administration, minibus driving, cleaning, etc. The partnership explains the name of Cookson's. Two full-time staff work as drivers/fitters and there is a pool of part-time drivers mainly for weekday school contracts plus several others available for weekend duties. All fitting is carried out in house and great care is taken to purchase good second-hand units. The workshop is the original agricultural engineering shed erected around 1972.

The current school contracts are Welshpool to Llanfair for the Welsh medium education (all schools teach Welsh as a second language with all other subjects in English, Welsh medium education teaches much of the curriculum in Welsh) and Churchstoke, Montgomery, Berriew and Garthmyl, all to Welshpool High School. Smaller buses feed to Abermule Primary School and minibuses act as feeders. The diary shows the variety of excursion work for the following week. Weekday work included Welshpool Horticultural Society to Highgrove, Gloucester (Prince of Wales estate); two school trips to Erddig (National Trust) near Wrexham; funeral party from Caersws to Pencoed (South Wales); a school trip to outdoor activities at Lake Vyrnwy; midibus to Manchester United and three midibuses for golfers and to Ludlow races. The weekend has a trial stage service called Spare Wheels, Welshpool Ladies Football away game, excursion to Llandudno and full bus to Ludlow Races and three evening vehicles for a Charity Ball evening at Llanfair. Mike also takes Welshpool Football Club on their away trips in the Welsh Premier League and has special panels for this duty. He will also help Wyn Lloyd of Machynlleth at short notice. He had taken on several of Wyn's excursions so that Wyn could deploy his coaches on rail replacement due to the cave collapse at Friog on the Cambrian line. Note that some of these trips such as away day golf, bowls, races, etc. often hire so the members can enjoy a drink without infringing drink-driving legislation. Mike recalls the Welshpool companies. The longest established company with a contining major interest in car retailing is Ballards. They ceased coach operation in the late 1980s. Derwen Lloyd operated in the 1950s with Bedford OBs and a parrot. Harry Evans continues with school contracts. Reflexion Coaches operated in the 1980s. There may have been others before Mike's childhood recall of the late 1980s. Pre-war companies included Tudors, Williams & Morris and finally W. Davies of Leighton.

The Bedford YMP crosses the bridge over the Afon Efyrnwy at Pont-llogel on an experimental Saturday service called 'Spare Wheels'. The route worked from Welshpool on a long loop to encourage Saturday travel linking towns such as Llanfair, Llanfyllin and Welshpool to smaller villages. The experiment was withdrawn after the trial period. The only stage service is a Monday to Friday Post Bus. MWM had a service from Llanerfyl to Llanfyllin on the last Thursday of each month to Pont-llogel. It was a 'thin' service even in the late 1940s. *Author (2005)*

The short body Bedford YMP stops at Llanfyllin town centre on the 'Spare Wheels' experiment. Tri-centrol had experimented with an 8 metre Bedford midi-bus. Bedford valued the design and decided to build in house. Only about 20 were built before General Motors decided to withdraw commercial manufacture from the UK. So this may be the last of a long line of Bedfords that served Montgomeryshire for over 75 years. The rota driver, Richard Carter called this route the Postman Pat run. *Author (2005)*

Edgar Owen and the Berriew Coaches

Berriew is one of the larger parish areas in the county with a compact central village. Much of the farmland is good. There are therefore a number of smaller groups within the immediate area. Examples are Revel, Brithdir, Garthmyl, Halfway and Brooks. Some of these are close to the canal and aqueduct that passes on the edge of the village. The aber (confluence) of the Afon Rhiw enters the Severn and the village is on the northern valley side. The Rhiw has settlements that would have an affinity with the village and these include Rhiewport, Felindre, Pant-y-ffridd and Manafon. The nearest station was Montgomery; the railway was built on the southern side of the Severn. The station is a classic example of why buses took so much custom in the 1920s as the station, with only a few surrounding houses, is two miles from both Montgomery and Berriew. Various light railway proposals were never pursued.

The village therefore has a catchment area of over 3,000 people. It continues to be served by eight stage buses each way between Llanidloes and Shrewsbury. The companies were Cookson's in the 1920s/30s, Mid-Wales Motorways from 1937 to 1969, then Crosville until the late 1980s, followed by Midland Red, Arriva Midland North and Tanat Valley Motors currently.

Edgar Owen was born in 1931. The family story is almost a copybook classic for a country bus story. Grandfather William Thomas was a wheelwright/blacksmith. Somewhere around 1905, he moved to Revel and started to supplement income with cycle repairs and sales. (Revel is from the Welsh word 'yr efail' meaning smithy.) The first car for hire (taxi) commenced duty in 1913. The sale of both petrol and paraffin had commenced from Pratts cans. Edgar's father Tom returned from the Great War. He had served in the Service Corps and had acquired both driving and fitting skills. He rejoined his father and brother John in the business. Lorry purchase commenced and a vehicle bought in 1920 was converted for the carriage of passengers to markets and other places. A 14-seat Ford was purchased in 1923. W.T. Owen and Sons were successfully trading with garage, haulage and bus service. There was a Monday service from Pant-y-ffridd down the Rhiw valley to Welshpool and a similar service to Newtown on Tuesday. The company had the first-ever contract with Montgomeryshire Education Committee to bring children in to the County Primary and also to the County Grammar at Welshpool. The children were put in a stock lorry if the bus was out of service. A 20-seat Bedford with a Thurgood body was purchased in 1932. Edgar can remember the Bedford when he was a child. It was packed with market goods and passengers during the war.

The business was to expand after the 1944 Education Act as the all-age schools ceased and all children aged 11 or over were taken to Welshpool Grammar and Secondary or the County Technical School at Newtown. Later there was a Comprehensive High School at Welshpool and the Further Education College at Newtown for some of those over 15. There were few cars with petrol rationing, so excursion traffic and weekends and school holidays boomed. Sunday School trips were still a very important part of the culture of Berriew and the surrounding villages. Boys from Saint Beuno's church purchased the *Beano* at Rhyl. All bus companies had difficulty in meeting

The flimsy Ford bus is being driven by John Owen (Edgar's uncle) in the late 1920s. The passengers are Garthmyl Rovers football team on an away fixture. The body would appear fixed to the chassis. Some were just a box that could be bolted to the flat lorry so that the lorry could be used for goods and passengers. The calendar heading dates from 1928 and indicates some of the services offered. Note that the nearest station location was still important.

Edgar Owen, Berriew

The Pant-y-ffridd bus arrives at Halfway near Garthmyl on the Tuesday market day return from Newtown *circa* 1933. The bus is a Bedford WLB Thurgood body with 20 seats. This bus would be the mainstay of World War II traffic with excess loading and infrequent service.

Edgar Owen, Berriew

Edgar stands by the Bedford Plaxton in the Revel yard in October 1977. The canal runs to the left of the building. The photograph was taken by Malcolm Yeoman on a test visit for the Vehicle Operation and Services Agency. *Edgar Owen, Berriew*

The Ford Transit in Welshpool has been highly polished and bunting hangs across the street. The passengers are the local dignatories on their way to Powis Castle to have lunch with the Earl and the Queen. *Edgar Owen, Berriew*

Cookson's bus draws through the centre of Berriew on the Welshpool to Newtown service. The flags are out so the picture is likely to be either the Jubilee of King George V (1935) or the Coronation of King George VI (1937). *Edgar Owen, Berriew*

An Arriva Midlands North bus arrives to cross the bridge over the river in Berriew at 11.39 am on the stage route between Shrewsbury and Llanidloes. *Author (2005)*

demand. Prailes of Hereford managed to secure a Bedford OWB Utility from Ireland. The bus was fitted with austerity wooden slatted seats and was used for a few months before Prailes had the material to fit upholstered seats.

Edgar took on an increasing role as both father and uncle aged. The fleet continued to be Bedfords but size increased from 29 to 36/41 to 53 seats. The final fleet had a 57-seat DAF Plaxton for the larger contracts. A minibus was used on school contracts and private hire work. Neither of the daughters or their respective husbands had a desire to take on the succession so Edgar opted to retire in 1998. The garage and the buses were sold to separate companies. Edgar still drives on a part-time basis for Worthen Motors on school contracts.

Edgar has retained certain correspondence of the company and a selection of examples follows.

Montgomeryshire and District Bus and Road Haulage Association, 1933 and 1934. The main objective was to assist all bus operators with problems arising from the Road Traffic Act, 1930. One sentence desires to obtain equal rights with the wealthier companies and the Traffic Commissioners. Subscription was based on ownership of PSV licences, examples being £1 1*s.* for one, £1 11*s.* 6*d.* for two and £2 2*s.* for three. Negotiations for a district agreement suggest a co-ordination of timetables, fares and contracts. It suggests an operating cost of 14-seats at 9*d.* per mile, 20-seats at 1*s.*, 26-seats at 1*s.* 3*d.* and 32-seats at 1*s.* 6*d.* and that these are charged when one operator assists another.

Correspondence sent and received from the Traffic Commissioners at Manchester, 1933. W.R. Davies requests that his company has the rights for Berriew due to Owens having an old bus and the population catchment area is low. Owens then objected stating the information submitted was incorrect and that they had purchased a bus in 1932 and the total catchment area was over 3,000 and not the 400 that was the immediate area around the depot. Various people including the headmaster, the justice of peace and the county councillor gave their support. W.R. Davies was to withdraw and he built up a far larger business at Welshpool and also at Newtown as the main Ford dealership in the county.

Road Services licence details to operate excursions and tour traffic, 1969. Examples of details include the following. Only one coach authorized on any one day. Only pre-booked passengers can be carried. Journeys to originate from Revel, Berriew, Forden, Brooks, Garthmyl, Montgomery and Castle Caereinion only. Routes are prescribed for Blackpool, Llandudno, Manchester, New Brighton, Rhyl and Aberystwyth with set parking and put-down/pick-up points. There were also restrictions into Shrewsbury for excursions not to operate before 7.00 pm. Special parking places were given for Manchester including football grounds such as Maine Road and for theatres including Belle Vue.

The Churchstoke salient with Bill Hailstone and his buses

Churchstoke and the related parishes such as Hyssington is almost an island of Wales within England. It is the only place where one can look east from England into the hills of Wales. All main A and B roads have to cross a patch of England to get to Churchstoke. There is evidence of human habitation over the centuries with carns, stone circles etc. to more recent Norman motte and bailey churches and a host of small non-conformist chapels. There are relics of mineral mines and it is not far to the narrow gauge Snailbeach railway from Crowsnest mine to the Minsterley interchange. This was still *in situ* (just) in the late 1940s.

Right: The poor image shows Dad (Bill Hailstone) on right and Mr R. Carpenter on the left in the early 1930s. The make of bus is unknown but note the clear view of the ladder and roof rack that was a permanent fixture on many small rural buses.

The Hailstone family

Below: Dad is the driver as his Bedford waits in Shrewsbury toward the end of World War II before negotiating the narrow lanes connecting a number of hamlets in West Shropshire before crossing into the Churchstoke parish. Vincent Greenhous of Shrewsbury built the narrow width body.

The Hailstone family and The Omnibus Society

The planned railways were never completed and the Bishops Castle Railway from Craven Arms terminated at Lydham Heath and reversed to Bishops Castle. The parish has two upland blocks split by the River Camlad. The river is unique as it flows from England into Wales and enters the Severn near Forden. The ancient drovers route on the Kerry Ridgeway is to the south of the village. Offa's Dyke crosses from south to north. Both routes are now part of long distance footpaths.

Heath Hailstone, the youngest of three children, recalls his father's buses. Heath has also consulted Arthur and Jennifer to ensure the greatest accuracy. Bill was born in 1909 and his childhood was spent in Bishops Castle. He commenced work for Vincent Greenhous at a small garage in the town. The Greenhous Group would expand to be one of the largest retailers in the Marches with the General Motors franchise for Vauxhall and Bedford. Bill was soon driving any vehicle and this would include the Greenhous charabanc. No driving licence was required in the late 1920s. Bill transferred his allegiance to Mr R. Carpenter with a network of bus services around Bishops Castle including Churchstoke. Bill decided to go independent in 1935 and purchased the Bedford UJ 9058 chassis from Vincent Greenhous. He arranged for a body to his own specification with roof rack, rear ladder and other features including a narrow width. The business worked from the rented yard at the rear of the Coach House Tavern at Churchstoke.

Bill received military call-up papers around 1940 but then immediately became exempt. He had just received the contract to carry miners to the collieries in the Wellington area. There was a tradition of mineral mining skills in this border area. The single Bedford worked very hard through the war years. It was still parked in a corner of Churchstoke as a rotting hulk in 1960. The company expanded its base after 1945 and a summary of duties by 1950 follows.

A stage route ran on Tuesday, Wednesday and three services on Saturday from Churchstoke via Old Churchstoke, Priest Weston etc. to Shrewsbury. There was a Churchstoke to Welshpool bus on Monday only. There was a struggle with the Traffic Commissioners to get any other work including the Bishops Castle to Newtown route. The only addition was the Saturday evening only service to Bishops Castle for the cinema. The colliery duty continued after the war. Excursion traffic was important with Sunday Schools, seaside days and shopping outings to Birmingham, Hereford, or Chester. The most interesting trip, sometimes requiring two buses, was to the Stiperstones Heaths to collect whimberries. The village was then full of ladies with ladles stirring the purple fluid in copper pots for jam. Bill was a very keen motor sports enthusiast, both cars and motorbikes. He therefore arranged many trips to Oulton Park, Aintree and Silverstone circuits plus the grass tracks near Bridgnorth, the Hawkstone scramble and the hill climbs such as at Loton near Criggion. Peter Rees worked with the author. Peter helped Bill organize these trips and recalls that they were well subscribed and lovely days out. School contracts expanded to both Welshpool and Bishops Castle for secondary education. It was the loss of some of these contracts that caused Bill to sell out in 1960. He worked for various garages both locally and then in Shrewsbury until he retired.

Heath recalls that the fleet peaked in the late 1940s when he was still at school. The fleet contained the original Bedford WTB, three OBs (Utility, a

Bill Hailstone worked for Carpenters before setting up his own business. The OWB has wartime headlight cowlings and wood slot indicator for Churchstoke. Carpenter operated a number of services around Bishops Castle including daily services to Newtown and market day specials.
The Omnibus Society

Bill Hailstone stands by his half-cab Crossley on an excursion to Llandudno with the Great Orme in the background. Heath can just remember that his father was not too happy with the Crossley diesel engine which was noted for leaking sump oil. *The Hailstone family*

Three buses in the Churchstoke yard. The centre bus is the Maudslay SF40. This was an early attempt to increase capacity. Heath can remember that the engine cowling would heat almost like an Aga. Passengers entering would put their hand on it to talk to dad and then jump back with the warmth. *The Hailstone family*

There is still a service only on Wednesday from Churchstoke to Shrewsbury. This service is very indirect proceeding through a number of settlements. The service is now operated by Boultons of Church Stretton with an Optare bus. The driver, Winston Ward, has driven along the border at Snead and turns at the Pottery in Churchstoke before heading into the lanes. One elderly lady boarding could remember the same route with Bill Hailstone when she was a teenager. *Author (2005)*

Three buses were timed to meet at Montgomery in the early 1950s. The first Bedford OB bus is to return to Newtown, the second is to return to Welshpool. Both were in MWM livery. The bus by the Town Hall was then a divison of MWM known as Worthen & District and waits to depart for Shrewsbury. *David Hughes, Shrewsbury*

Worthen Travel's coach waits beside the town hall in Montgonery prior to departure at 9.45 am to Shrewsbury. There are three services daily with alterations and extras for school term and Saturdays only. Arriva Midlands North also provide a further service at 5.45 pm to Shrewsbury. An elderly lady tapped on Brian's shoulder with the advice that if he just waited a few minutes, he would have a far better view of the historic townhall without the bus. *Author (2005)*

Duple coach and a Duple bus), two half-cabs (Crossley and Dennis) and a full front Maudslay SF40.

The original small Bedford bus is still recalled. Anyone waiting to catch it would either wait or put a tea towel or enamel bowl in the hedge so the bus would stop! The bus carried much farm produce and Bill or one of the other drivers would use their spare time at Welshpool or Shrewsbury to do some tasks such as paying bills for some of the older villagers. The bus could carry a coffin and the mourners. One lady had purchased a precious new bike. This was placed on the roof rack but was missing between Priest Weston and Old Churchstoke. The bus immediately returned along the very narrow lane to find the bike hanging on an oak branch. The owner with his little Bedford had become a lifeline for the community in the period of 1935 to 1950. It is sad that the mobility of the car should remove such a way of life.

Worthen Motors

David Pye is from Llandyssil (Montgomery) and attended Penygloddfa Secondary Modern School in Newtown before the comprehensive high school. He would travel daily to school on one of the MWM Bedford OBs. He started to work for the Owen Brothers at the Revel Garage, Berriew, after he had completed National Service. Edgar Owen would have been a similar age and they have been firm friends for many years. David learned the skills of a garage mechanic on lorries, coaches and cars. He soon passed his PSV test. Tom Green worked as an administrator for MWM at the Newtown office. Worthen Motors was the last company to come into Mid-Wales in 1945 and they retained their Shropshire identification as Worthen and District Motor Service Ltd. Tom asked David to join him as driver/fitter in 1963 when the Worthen section was purchased from the receivers. David took on duties as manager within a few years at the request of the family when Tom became unwell. David was offered the business but could not afford it. The business was transferred to Valley Motors (ex-Carpenters) of Bishops Castle so David continued as the Worthen manager. David applied for a school contract in the Montgomery area and was successful. Peter Lewis of Valley Motors suggested that David take on the complete Worthen section. David had now inherited some property and decided to use it as collateral in addition to a bank loan so he was now owner. He took on the stage route of Montgomery to Shrewsbury, more school contracts and the expanded services became the foundation of the current company expanding on the site of the Minsterley station yard that had closed in 1965.

The historical route of Shrewsbury to Montgomery has a minimum of three services daily, except Sundays, and is the shift for one bus and one driver. Worthen Motors has substantial secondary school contracts to both Shropshire and Powys. It includes a bus for Newtown and one for Welshpool High School, four buses to Church Stretton, two to Bishops Castle and one to Minsterley.

The company hires to the National Express franchise providing the weekend and summer supplement on the Shrewsbury to London route once the

Right: The then young David Pye, seen on the left, and his boss, Tom Green, in the centre have driven to Blackpool in a car. The Duple representative hands over the documentations and David drove the new coach back to Worthen and Tom returned in the car. Bill Cross collected a new Duple at Hendon in London in 1945. The Duple factory moved to the Burlingham site at Blackpool in the 1960s. *David Pye, Worthen Travel*

Below: The AEC Reliance Duple was purchased from Jones of Aberbeeg. Tom Green purchased it for the ex-Mid-Wales Motorways route from Montgomery to Shrewsbury. It is seen in Shrewsbury in July 1969. *David Pye and the Omnibus Society*

The Midland Red Leyland National with National Bus Company logo prepared to travel east from Shrewsbury while the Worthen Travel Bedford waits to commence the stage route to Montgomery. *David Pye, Worthen Travel*

Fords were not the commonest of coaches but they were good value. The Ford with the school bus insignia is parked in the Minsterley yard. *David Pye, Worthen Travel*

Above: The white DAF Bermuda is parked at Welshpool. It has been used on contract from Llandyssil/Montgomery to Welshpool High School. The driver will often be the retired Edgar Owen of Berriew. David's career started with Edgar's father and uncle in the early 1950s. All companies arrange to park school contract buses to minimize dead time travel rather than return to the main depot daily.

Author (2005)

Right: David Pye stands by the Van Hool being prepared for hire to National Express to supplement the Aberystwyth and Wrexham weekend and holiday peaks onward from Shrewsbury to London. There is little evidence that this yard was the terminus for goods and passengers on the Minsterley branch. David has now worked for over 45 years in the coach industry at Berriew and Worthen.

Author (2005)

Aberystwyth and Wrexham coaches are full from either Shrewsbury or Telford. Up to three executives may be employed on this in July/August.

Local private hire is constant with schools and various local societies. Sunday school bookings are far less common than they were 40 years ago. They have been replaced by clubs, especially pensioners and their days out. Most Saturdays will see a coach or more going to a football premier league ground.

The current fleet is around 20 with one 11 seat mini, one 33-seat midi and all the others are 51 to 57 seats. The fleet is based on DAFs with Cummins engines. There are six full time drivers/fitters and around 12 part-timers. There is full time help with administration including David's daughter.

David inherited two vintage buses (*see illustrations*). Demand for a good vintage bus can be excellent so they were cashed in as a modern coach can earn more. David's hobby is military vehicles and he has AEC, Leyland and Canadian Ford lorries from the 1940s, a Wilys jeep, a post-war Austin Champ and a self-propelled tracked gun. He and several friends enjoy a day at a rally.

There is now little evidence that the bus depot is on the site of the railway station and goods yard but evidence of the track can easily be seen at various points on the way to Shrewsbury. David has some interesting documents that include the full timetable for MWM, January 1955 and the fleet history of the Independent Stage Carriage Operators of Shropshire, 1971. The latter includes routes that overlap into Montgomeryshire from Bishops Castle and Oswestry so it includes Parish, Hampsons and Vaggs. David has a good collection of photography from the MWM connection to the present day but only a small selection is possible in this volume.

Vaggs was a coach company at Knockin near Oswestry. EUJ 787 was a Perkins engine Thornycroft with a Churchill body. It is stated to be parked in Welshpool in 1960 (although this may be an error in the narrative and could be Oswestry). Vaggs only Montgomeryshire stage route travelled a few yards in Wales at Llanymynech before proceeding to Shrewbury via Kinnerley, closely following the long closed light railway route. *David Pye, Worthen Travel*

David inherited the ex-Southdown Leyland from Tom Green and continued to run the vehicle for vintage use. It is seen parked at a vintage rally. The steamroller was very important in the 1920s, Pritchards Transport being a local concern. The light rural buses ran on poor surface minor roads based on crushed stone with surface maintained by regular rolling. *David Pye, Worthen Travel*

David Pye purchased this Bedford OB from a preservation society in 1987. It was one of the ex-MWM buses that had taken him to school in Newtown in the early 1950s. The bus regained the PSV licence and was used to collect children in the Chirbury area and then worked as vintage transport in the summer between sites of the Ironbridge Museum complex near Telford. It is seen close to the River Severn in the Coalbrookdale Gorge close to the famous pioneer Ironbridge world heritage site. *David Hughes, Shrewsbury*

Chapter Nine

Local Photographic Collections

Several people have collected their own record of the buses and coaches in the locality over the years. Some of these such as Harry Beadles and Morris Brothers of Tanat Valley have already been included.

It is an impossible task to select from substantial collections. The research is the opposite from that faced by the author searching for material for his book on the Mawddwy, Van and Kerry branch lines where any original image was scarce.

A Montgomeryshire man works a career with Midland Red

David Hughes was brought up in Pontrobert. This is a small village between Llanfair Caereinion and Llanfyllin. He was one of the sons living at the village store. David travelled daily to Llanfair on a MWM bus based at the Llanfair depot. The driver was Dic Williams who lived at Pontrobert. The Bedford, usually an OB in the early 1950s, would be parked overnight at Pontrobert. The bus would do the school duty and then be used for Welshpool (Mondays), Oswestry (Wednesdays) and Llanfair fair (monthly) market day with timetabled return just before school collection. The same bus would travel light to Four Crosses and operate the then Saturday-only service to Shrewsbury via Crew Green. David's late mother would have travelled from Llanymynech to Shrewsbury on the Col Stephens light railway route. This would have been on the Ford bus chassis back-to-back railcar employed in a desperate attempt in the late 1920s to keep the system viable. David recalls that his mother found the converted buses had an uncomfortable ride compared with the GWR coach from Llanymynech to Oswestry. The wheel flanges were very noisy on the rails and everything rattled and vibrated.

Buses continued to interest David as he helped in the village shop in 1960. He therefore applied to Midland Red and was taken on as a conductor. He took his PSV test at the age of 21 at the Midland Red School at Bearwood. He was to drive for several years prior to becoming a car driver instructor for the Kenning Group. He returned to Midland Red in 1969. He started his photographic collection of bus operation about this time and usually had the camera in the cab to record anything unusual.

Midland Red only had a minor role in any travel within Mid-Wales such as cross hire with Crosville in an emergency. MWM was struggling to maintain the Newtown to Shrewsbury service so the operational licence was transferred to Crosville around 1970 and Crosville buses started to appear in the Shrewsbury bus station. All became part of the National Bus Company around 1970. Midland Red was split into four operational divisions and Shropshire was part of Midland Red North. The West Midland conurbation became part of the area Passenger Transport Executive in 1974 and this saw the demise of the

The Dennis J3s were purchased new by Merthyr Tydfil Urban District in 1952 with a locally built D.J. Davies body with rear entrance for conductor operation. Four or five were purchased by MWM in 1959 and converted to single person operation. The rear section was rebuilt and the door inserted with mechanical linkage from the driver's cabin. It was an awkward system. This bus was one of several that were sold to Reed & Mallik to be used as works buses from Welshpool, Newtown and Rhayader during the construction of the Clywedog dam.

David Hughes Collection

Bedford MLM 384 was on the MWM inventory of 1957. The Marshall Mulliner body was on an SB chassis and was an ex-UKAEA (Atomic Energy) works bus. The company hoped to market this extended body to replace the popular but obsolete OB. John James (*see Crosville section, Chapter Fourteen*) took his PSV test so this bus may have been allocated to the Llanfair depot. One of the Guy double-deckers is parked behind on the site of the then Shrewsbury bus station.

David Hughes Collection

Transport House was used as the Head Office for MWM from about 1948 to 1985. It is now an hotel. The garage on the left-hand side with Wolseley embossment was one of Cookson's garages in the 1930s. *David Hughes Collection*

The view is taken from the Rope Walk (named after an obsolete industry) looking to the locked door of the MWM service shed. The whole complex was built for the horse trade (cavalry and urban haulage) opening in 1914. The locomotive is hauling the summer evening direct service from Euston to Aberystwyth that ran from around 1979 to 1989. *David Hughes Collection*

Mid-Wales Motorways had two Bedford VALs for a short period. They were not really suited to short daily school contracts on many upland B roads. The coach is turning by the church of St Mary to avoid the congested Welshpool town centre. David would have been standing on what was the narrow gauge track between the main line station and the current terminus of Raven Square. *David Hughes Collection*

The MWM Bedford VAL is parked at the Welshpool depot besides a Crosville with a NBC logo on the radiator. The Crosville is EFM 180H and is one of the very successful Bristol RE series. *David Hughes Collection*

A510 HVT was the only MWM coach to operated within the National Express franchise. It was employed on the Shrewsbury to Leeds run. It is parked in Shrewsbury with a Midland Red bus in the background. *David Hughes Collection*

The Crosville Cymru Leyland Tiger with Duple Laser body squeezes through the congested centre of Welshpool in June 1989 with the driver cursing caravans! The by-pass would soon remove such chronic congestion every day with impossible delays during summer weekends. The National Express section of the NBC did not like the smaller coaches so these were returned to Crosville for limited excursion work etc. and that may explain the destination of 'Private'.
David Hughes Collection

The Oswestry depot has now transferred from Crosville Cymru to Midland Red. The Midland Red bus is ready to work one of the Newtown local services. The main depot will now be Shrewsbury with a sub-depot at Abermule. The smaller Mid Wales Travel Mercedes is again a town service but can work through to the housing on the northern side of the River Severn across the wrought-iron Long Bridge with its weight restriction. This date would be around 1993.

David Hughes Collection

Bedford YMT with Unicar body has been relegated to PSV L-plated training duties. It is parked in Newtown in 1992. A sister coach was parked in Machynlleth as the office as the bus station was then with a lease company. The Bedfords were acquired second-hand as many of the original Crosville buses had either moved to Crosville England or the directors/speculators had sold on and purchased older units to try and keep the company viable. The period of privatization for Crosville Cymru between 1986 and 1992 would now appear to be a very sad event for a company and a work force that had won high respect from the local community since 1924.

David Hughes Collection

F77 CJC was an Iveco with a Carlyle body with an unusual variation of having a rear luggage boot. It is about to cross the bridge over the Dyfi before crossing the flood plain into Machynlleth. A spirited effort was still being made to get the services suited to South Gwynedd and North Powys. The buses of Crosville Cymru were colourful in the early 1990s with what became known as the prancing dragon on the sides. *David Hughes Collection*

David Hughes stands by the Arriva Park and Ride service for Shrewsbury at the Oxon car park one week after retirement. He had started work for Midland Red in 1962 leaving the small village of Pontrobert in North Montgomeryshire. Oxon is the car park for the western catchment area so many Montgomeryshire people from Churchstoke in the south to Llanymynech in the north will make use of this service. *Author (2004)*

David Llewelyn Jones of Cyfronydd had an unusual Bristol with coach body photographed in the Cyfronydd yard in 1986. Bob Bowden started to assist as a driver in the early 1980s to help with farm income. *Graham Sharp*

Bob Bowden commenced his company based at Golfa when he purchased David Llewelyn Jones's company and his Mercedes. The coach company fits in with the duties of the family farm. Four of the family have PSV licences. The original Mercedes (in foreground) plus a Toyota Optimo and a Mercedes Vario are seen in the yard of Gelli Isaf in 2005. *Graham Sharp*

municipals of Wolverhampton, Walsall, West Bromwich, Birmingham and Coventry. The Crosville depot at Oswestry originated with Western Transport and was always thought of as Crosville operations in Wales. De-regulation started in the mid-1980s. All Midland Red services to Oswestry transferred to Crosville in 1986 and an out-station was established in Newtown. Crosville Cymru was in desperate financial straits so the Oswestry depot was rented to Midland Red North in 1991 and then purchased. Soon Midland Red buses were working services such as Oswestry/Welshpool and Shrewsbury/Llanidloes. Out-stations at Llanidloes and Welshpool closed. It was decided that the Llanidloes service would be easier to service from the Shrewsbury depot. David was asked if he would help out on this route during holidays and emergency as he had local knowledge and some understanding of the 'lingo'. He therefore found that he often would drive a rota in his home county.

David had to retire just before retirement age because the yearly medical picked up slight diabetes with potential eyesight difficulty. He was often employed on the Shrewsbury Park and Ride especially from Meole Brace serving Ludlow, Bridgnorth and Telford. Far more people from Montgomeryshire were likely to travel on either Chester or Shrewsbury Park & Ride than on their own county bus routes in 2005. David has worked most routes of Midland Red in Shropshire to such places as Oswestry, Hereford and Wolverhampton. He never worked from Oswestry into Wales on such routes as the Llangynog rail replacement now operated by Tanat Valley Coaches. The motorways witnessed the growth of long distance coaches and David would drive the then ME7 National Express Shrewsbury to London and the summer Saturday-only service to Llandudno. David has acquired much information and photography of MWM in the early post-war period and a fraction of this has been selected to support other sections in this volume. The author asked several of the older staff and it is recalled that several bus enthusiasts, including a rotund jovial man, often took pictures in the early 1950s and the prints were available to the staff.

The coach/bus manual called the 'The Little Red Book'

Graham Sharp was born in 1930 and brought up at Tamworth north of Birmingham. Geoffrey Hickson was a close school friend and Geoff's father owned one of the local bus companies. This friendship started a long interest in buses. Graham would spend many spare hours with Geoffrey in the coach depot. They would also have days out on excursions if several seats had not been sold.

Graham trained as an engineer and moved to the Newtown area to start his own small engineering company. He had been employed by a specialist company that manufactured windows and frames for the bus/coach industry prior to moving to Mid-Wales. His work was initial design prior to manufacture which was on another site. Much of the work was for Plaxtons, the coachbody builder at Scarborough. The company also worked on the initial design of the Leyland National. Graham recalls that there was a rattle in the middle of the bus

Harry Evans Coaches of Welshpool commenced operating coaches in 1968 and continues to the current date with school contracts, excursions etc. The photographs date from the early 1980s. The first shows a Bedford purchased from Hampsons Luxury Coaches of Oswestry.

Graham Sharp

A Dodge minibus is parked in the Welshpool depot. This would be part of the short-lived Chrysler Group when all Commers and Dodges were sold as Dodge. *Graham Sharp*

Trefaldwyn Motors operated a fleet of up to 18 vehicles based at Montgomery (Trefaldwyn is the Welsh for Montgomery). They ceased trading due to the ill health of the proprietor, Mr G.E.H. Price. The bus body is thought to be a Leyland Dominant. The destination board shows Ludlow. The A road from Newtown to Craven Arms and then on to Ludlow would be a natural daily bus route, if there were fewer cars, incorporating Kerry, Montgomery, Churchstoke, Lydham etc. *Graham Sharp*

Trefaldwyn Motors had a Commer and this marque was never common in Mid-Wales. Graham thought that this battered version was being held for restoration. *Graham Sharp*

Mantles of Trefeglwys retains a garage business and minibus feeder services for the isolated uplands into the area primary school at Trefeglwys. The Bova was the final coach sold on to Celtic Travel when Mantles opted out of the coach business. The previous coaches were Bedfords. *Graham Sharp*

Mrs Williams of Llangadfan had an unusual AEC with Harrington body. This coach was sold to a bus enthusiast when Mrs Williams opted to retire in 1996. *Graham Sharp*

Ballards of Welshpool continues trading as a retail dealer. The company was established in the 1920s and was the dealer for Beans cars and vans in the late 1920s. Their coach trade until the 1980s was mainly school contracts. The Bedford was sold on to Beadles of Newtown.

Graham Sharp

M.A. Jones vehicles parked in the yard at Llansilin. Llansilin was then in Clwyd but is now part of Powys. M.A. Jones had a substantial trade including stage routes that are now operated by Tanat Valley Coaches. The photograph shows two Bedfords and a Renault minibus.

Graham Sharp

John Jones of Crossgates/Pen-y-bont near Llandrindod owned a Commer. The Commer was purchased by Trefaldwyn Motors and restored to original colours and used for coach rallies. The two-stroke TS3 engine was the power source for this unit. *Graham Sharp*

The selection from Graham's collections was chosen mainly for companies that have ceased trading. As one goes out, another is always willing to start. Gold Star is a current Newtown company and two of their coaches are shown in a Newtown yard. *Graham Sharp*

and that the fault may have been with the window. Graham was sent to the test track at Leyland and had to sit in the bus when it travelled 100 laps at full speed, becoming dizzy. The fault was finally traced to a body fault and not the window and a slight alteration to one of the body support struts cured the fault.

Graham wrote to the editor of 'The Little Red Book' informing him that some of the information on Mid-Wales was not very accurate. He was asked, and accepted to undertake the task of annual updating for Mid-Wales and Shropshire. The Little Red Book is not all that little. It is considered as one of the leading directories for the bus and coach industry. It lists manufacturers, supplies and the operating companies.

So Graham started to make an annual pilgrimage. He has taken a camera with him and a small selection taken between 1975 and 2000 are included, many are from companies that have ceased trading.

L. Hughes of Llangyniew near Llanfair had a single coach in the early 1990s on school contract work. It is a Bedford 600m with a Duple Vista body. *Graham Sharp*

The bus was photographed on route from Pembroke to Bosworth. Vernon Evans is at the wheel and the bus is at the Frankwell area of Shrewsbury. Note 'Private' on the screen.

David Hughes Collection

The two bus drivers, Vernon Evans of MWM and Harriet Lewis (Maggie the bus) of the BBC pose in front of the radiator of the Bedford OB. The coach was not required every day. Vernon took his place as a part actor and poses dressed as a monk. *(Both) Ann Evans, Newtown*

Chapter Ten

The BBC film entitled *Bus to Bosworth*

The title follows the story of a contract of a coach and driver for one month from Mid-Wales Motorways to the British Broadcasting Corporation (BBC) at Cardiff. The BBC chartered a Bedford Duple Vista in July/August 1975. The purpose was for a historical drama documentary retracing the route taken by Henry Tudor following his landing at Dale (Pembrokshire) on Sunday 7th August, 1485. Both Henry and his militia then travelled through Wales and the English Midlands to battle with Richard III at Bosworth Field near Leicester. The opposing forces met on 21st August, 1485. The result was utter defeat for the 'Yorkist Forces'. Richard was slain still wearing his crown that Henry then placed on his own head to become King Henry VII.

The bus was driven by Maggie the bus (Miss Davies). Harriet Lewis played this role. The schoolmaster (Mr Meredith) was played by Kenneth Griffith and the schoolmistress (Miss Evans) was Rachel Thomas. All three were highly skilled and well known within both languages of Welsh broadcasting. The older children of Pontardawe Welsh Language Primary School occupied the coach. They must have enjoyed the month taking part in the film for their enthusiasm shines on every frame. The background music and songs are those from the Welsh entertainer, Max Boyce.

The film shows Harriet in the close up speech roles but the distance shots including the coach moving shows a lady in the same dress, but with a hidden PSV licence as it was Vernon Evans wearing a wig! A letter from the BBC to MWM thanks the company for providing the two 'stars' of the film, the vintage bus and Vernon. Vernon smiles his way through every adversary. He was splendid company so both the BBC staff and the Pontardawe children enjoyed his skill and kindness immensely.

So a filmed journey took place from Dale to Bosworth using a mode of transport of another age, but with a vehicle that already was vintage chosen for the assignment. The direct 174 mile single journey (Henry Tudor did not have a return ticket) was expanded to a very roundabout 1,400 miles for an inclusive contract price of £450. The BBC was to cover accommodation and food costs for the driver. The filming eventually involved mileage of 2,000, and many extra hours for Vernon, so a supplementary contract invoice for £168 was issued.

The film opens with Henry Tudor coming in from the sea and making his way up the beach to the waiting coach at Dale. The coach then proceeds on the journey with other school staff and the children. It passes a cromlech on the Preseli Mountains and stops at Y Wern that is a Tudor house. Already the problems of a school trip intertwine with the Tudor story as the children want ice cream, they need to go to the toilet and the bus driver wants to have a 'fag'. The coach proceeds up the Cardigan coast area and shows the Aberystwyth promenade and the National Library. At Machynlleth, the coach passes the T Senedd (Welsh Parliament) of Owain Glyndŵr. Much of the route is on quieter B roads. In Montgomeryshire, it passes two historical sites of Mathrafal near

Meifod and Gregynog Hall near Tregynon, before crossing the border close to the Breidden Hills near Criggion. The coach enters Shrewsbury passing through the Tudor section of the town and then proceeds towards Newport across the Shropshire plain. Then the coach proceeds along the motorway between Wolverhampton and Birmingham before heading to Bosworth. Here the children enact the battle. The final shots show the teachers exhausted from looking after the children, the children tired of being questioned and the coach driver fed up with everyone. The coach then leaves the park at Bosworth and started the long return run back to Wales. The film was shown on the Welsh Network at Christmas 1975. It then appeared on the national network in early 1976 and repeats have been shown again during the last decades. It is a lovely film and the specialist highlight must be the internal and external shots of the Bedford OB with the unique transmission whine as it trundles over hill and dale.

Accommodation was arranged for Vernon at Dale (20th to 23rd July), Pontardawe (24th July to 3rd August), Aberystwyth (4th to 6th August) Edgbaston (10th August) and finally Burbage near Bosworth (11th to 14th August). The bus was not required on certain days as filming took place with sets.

Ann, the daughter of the late Vernon Evans, now recalls some of her father's duties with MWM including access to his photographic collection. Vernon was born in 1920 and was brought up in the then intense Welsh speaking area of Pontrobert within the family farm. He joined the army when he was 18 just before World War II and served a long period in South Africa and acquired some proficiency in one of the languages, probably Xhosa. He returned to the family farm and became a very keen member of the Territorial Army and received honours for this service. He started to supplement income from the small farm by bus driving for MWM, either from their Llanfair or Welshpool depot in the early 1950s. He became full time based at Newtown around 1955 so the family moved to the Garthowen Estate. Ann was born in Newtown and has clear memories from both the Primary School and the High School trips when Dad would often be the driver.

The company asked him if he would do the month duty for the film. The coach called at Newtown and Ann can remember Kenneth Griffith visiting their home for a cup of tea. Dad received a degree of leg-pulling because he had to dress up as 'Maggie the bus'. The family sat around the television to see the film and Dad had kept the wig and put it on. Maybe everyone has an ability to act. There were several days where the bus or coach was not needed and Dad took part as an extra including that of a monk. The future son of Henry VII was not noted for his kindness to the monks of Strata Florida and Strata Marcella and the coach would have passed close to the sites of these destroyed Cistercian Abbeys.

Dad was driving the lead bus of two between Welshpool and Newtown in 1982. The other driver noticed the front bus was tracking erractically and signalled for everyone to draw in. Dad was starting to have a stroke. He recovered his speech and mobility with considerable determination but his PSV licence was withdrawn. He died in 1992. Ann knows that he would be thrilled to realise that someone is researching a facet of his bus-driving career.

Poor royal Richard became a fatality at Bosworth. The coach had greater luck and has never reached the terminus as it is still in operation. Terry Jones purchased MFM 39 for preservation just after the coach had taken part in the film in the autumn of 1975. The coach was christened 'Bosworth'. Terry was only 20 and he was too young to have a licence for the vehicle. He was legally entitled to drive it by 1976 and started taking it to vintage rallies. The coach underwent much restoration throughout the 1980s and was recertified for PSV duties in 1986. At this point, Terry turned his hobby into a business and formed the beginning of Vista Coaches at Yatton near Bristol. The company now has a series of older coaches and provides a service of tours. The Bosworth bus is a treasured possession and continues to be used every season.

Right: Commer introduced light buses to compete with the successful Bedfords. This photograph was taken during World War II outside the Chandos in Knighton town centre. This bus and others would have worked their way to Newtown as well as to the surrounding villages around Knighton.
The Omnibus Society

The company owned numerous Bedford OBs. This has an unusual entry door. It had AZ on the registration plate as it was second-hand from Northern Ireland Railways. Note the Duple OB in the background.
The Owen family, Knighton

Chapter Eleven

The Market day-only services

Bus services for market days were an immediate feature of all independents as they established their services in the 1920s. Buses with goods and country folk made their way from every corner of the county to the respective market. These would include Welshpool, Newtown, Oswestry, Shrewsbury, Machynlleth, Dolgellau and Bishops Castle as well as monthly smaller village fairs. These services started to be curtailed as farmers acquired their own vehicles but a number of services still remained in 2005. Newtown maintains a large street fair on Tuesdays and a smaller fair on Saturdays. This dates back to when the town was established in 1279 and was referred to as Nova Villa in Norman French. A number of photographs of some of the services are included with a detailed record of one company and its route.

Owens of Knighton is a Radnorshire Company. The narrative has been given by David who is one of the three of the current generation along with Liz and Tom. The Welsh name for Knighton is Tref-y-clawdd. The translation of 'town on Offa's Dyke' describes the geographical situation. Owens has its office in Wales but the bus yard is across the River Teme in England. The company was founded in 1897. Arthur Owen, great grandfather of the current Directors, worked with horses using traps and a wagonette. Much of the trade centred on Knighton railway station. An automobile was purchased prior to World War I. The work also included that of a common carrier. A pantechnicon was still operating for furniture removal until the early 1960s.

The first charabanc (French for carriage with benches) was purchased in the early 1920s. A Tuesday and Saturday service to Newtown was soon established so the service has a continuous history of 80 years plus within the same family. There was a skirmish with Yeomans of Hereford to establish routes in the Upper Teme valley in the 1930s. Grandad presented his case to the Traffic Commissioners and it was decided that the potential traffic only warranted a single operating company. The route would maintain up to five journeys at the peak between 1930 and 1950. Stage routes were across three divisions. Knighton to Ludlow was in the Midlands, Knighton to Presteigne was in South Wales and Knighton to Newtown was in North West. The Traffic Commission allocated the main business to the 'Primary' (maybe the Midlands) and the other two were called 'Backings'. David Owen can just remember the redundant gantry in the yard. This would change the body of a lorry that could be used as a flat, a 20-seat bus, a van or a hearse; Buckinghams of Birmingham built the system. David recalls travel to Newtown when he was a child in the 1950s He would help the then driver, Alf Wright, load bread, meat and fresh fruit/vegetables. Alf collected the passengers on the journey through the Upper Teme Valley but also unloaded the goods to the shops that were then present in every settlement. Parcels etc. would be collected in Newtown and then unloaded on the afternoon return journey.

The current fleet has nine coaches, four minibuses and two hospital cars. There is a full time staff of five and a pool of around 10 part-time drivers. The

The Bedford CF van replaced the CA van and was soon adapted as a minibus as there was adequate headroom. It competed well with the Transit and the Sherpa in the 1970s. NFO 202R is the smaller 12-seat version and is at a local sports fete in the Knighton area.

The Owen family, Knighton

The then-young Tom and David, now the Directors, stand as juniors in front of a Bedford Production YRQ Plaxton Panorama Elite. This coach became the top selling single-deck sale in the early 1970s and was the ideal replacement for an independent with a rural route. Some were sold to divisions of the National Bus Company. Ivor Parish recalls that the entry door was air powered and worked with perfection except in very low temperatures when moisture condensed to freeze the valves. *The Owen family, Knighton*

Numerous second-hand Bedfords were purchased through the 1950s to the 1990s. 731 DWC was a standard VAM with a Duple Bella Venture body with the 330 Bedford diesel engine.

The Owen family, Knighton

Owens' coach leaves Newtown on the Tuesday fair day. It passes under the Dolfor Bridge on the journey to Knighton at 2.30 pm. The late-running Arriva train (17 minutes late) heads to Machynlleth. The bridge is close to the River Severn at 114 metres above sea level (asl). The coach now commences a continuous gradient for 7 miles to Crugynnau at 470 metres asl.

Author (2005)

The Churchstoke to Shrewsbury Wednesday-only service pulls through the narrow lanes of the scattered settlement of Old Churchstoke/Hen Ystog on the edge of Rowton and Corndon Hills. The Optare is provided by Boultons of Church Stretton. *Author (2005)*

The Pontrobert to Oswestry Wednesday-only 9.30 am service starts by the church. The Mercedes is provided by Parish Minibuses. The driver for the day was Ivor Parish who was the previous owner of the company and he helps the new owners. This was a service by Mid-Wales Motorways in the 1950s. *Author (2005)*

Owens' coach arrives on the high moorland having completed the long climb from Newtown. Cilfaesty Hill is in the background and is the highest point on the Kerry Ridgeway at 528 metres. Three rivers start on this high watershed. The Mule enters the Severn to the east of Newtown, the Teme enters the Severn at Worcester and the River Ithon joins the Wye at Newbridge and the Wye merges into the Severn estuary at Chepstow. *Author (2005)*

company tries to standardize the current coach fleet on Cummins Paramounts for simplicity. The business is based on school contracts, excursions/private hire and tours. The first school contract goes back to the 1920s for the transfer of scholarship children to the then long-established John Beddoes Grammar School at Presteigne. The company has a daily term time bus to Coleg Powys in Newtown and a minibus or car to the Cedewain Special School that is situated less than a mile from the college. The bus is parked all day at Newtown and the two drivers return to Knighton (am) and Newtown (pm) in the smaller vehicle. The only stage routes are now along the Upper Teme Valley with the Tuesdays-only service to Newtown (every fortnight in winter) and Thursdays only to Knighton fair. The Newtown bus carries up to 30 passengers but has an average of around 20. The usual driver is Jeanie Owen, the wife of Tom. The bus is almost a social cultural event rather like a portable eisteddfod. Many of the passengers would now be families from the fourth generation and their ancestors would have known great-grandfather Arthur Owen.

David has several literary descriptions of this bus service. One is called 'Over the Kerry Hills' and describes a day travelling on stage routes from Worcester, Kidderminster, Shrewsbury, Newtown, Knighton, Ludlow, Hereford and return to Worcester taking 13 hours to travel 180 miles. The second is by Cynric Mytton Davies in an article in the *Montgomeryshire County Times* in September 1971. Cynric recalls 'The Friendly Blue Bus' describing the route and the passengers. The bulk of the route is on the B4355. It was and remains a spectacular journey through little-known small villages of the high uplands on the Welsh side of the Marcher borders.

The author recalls certain winter days teaching at the Newtown site of Coleg Powys over the years. Heavy rain would start to turn to snow during the day. A request would come to staff to ensure that Knighton students made their way to the collection point as the bus would attempt to return over the Kerry Hill before the drifts closed in. Soon a similar request would follow for both Llandrindod and Llanfair Caereinion so the day would be abandoned. A small selection of the family photographs has been selected.

The Builth Wells, Rhayader, Newtown Tuesday-only service travels along where the railway track used to be on the final section of Llanidloes bypass. The old road that is now a park for the rugby club can be seen through the hedge. The Dennis coach is operated by Roy Brown Coaches of Builth Wells. Brown's have extensive operations in Radnor and Brecon but this is their only route into Montgomeryshire. *Author (2005)*

The Minsterley Motors coach left Pontesbury at 9.30 to travel via Minsterley, Lydham and Churchstoke to arrive at Newtown on Tuesdays only at 11.00 am. The older Volvo hurries between Sarn and Kerry. It collects up to 30 passengers with either Shropshire discount or Powys free passes. Minsterley Motors operates an interval service from Shrewsbury to Bishops Castle using new coaches with assistance from Shropshire County Council. The service runs along the border for about two miles near Whit Grit and Hyssington. *Author (2005)*

The Bishops Castle via the Clun Valley to Newtown Tuesday-only service is operated by Whittle from their depot at Ludlow. The company usual employs an Optare but the bus shown is an unusual unit. It is on a Dennis chassis with a special body that still retains double access doors at the rear. It was formerly a military hospital bus. The service fits a run back to Kerry at mid-day before leaving to Bishops Castle at 1.35 pm. Shropshire timetables list the service from Ludlow to Bishops Castle. This bus works along a single width B road with passing places and across open moor. The result is that the bus is often covered with rural grime by the time it arrives in Newtown coach park beside the Severn flood bank. Whittle's also run a Clun via Bishops Castle to Welshpool service on Mondays only. *Author (2005)*

The Mid Wales Travel runs a Tuesday-only service between Llanfair Caereinion and Newtown. MWM had a daily service plus several extra on both Tuesdays and Saturdays in the 1950s. The bus is crossing the new concrete bridge that replaced a narrow stone bridge over the Afon Rhiw close to Ystrad Uchaf. A proposed light railway from Cilgwrgan (Abermule) via Bettws, Tregynon, New Mills and Ystrad never proceeded further than a concept. The new bridge was necessary for heavy lorries working from a large quarry producing road stone, liquid cement for delivery and cut-stone for building. *Author (2005)*

The trial run on the Llanildoes-Llangurig route commenced on 4th February, 1967. Postman/driver Derek Jones entered the converted Morris LD Van. The Post Office was then still part of the GPO (mail and telephones). *The County Times*

The services on offer increased. This shows the Newtown to New Mills service in the early 1980s. Adapted versions of the Commer PB (or Dodge) minibuses became the common unit in the 1970s. Note the extra height gained by the fibreglass extension in the roof and note that the sign writing is now bilingual. *David Hughes, Shrewsbury*

Chapter Twelve

The Royal Mail Bus Services

Capital-intensive concepts that require a large user base arrive late, if at all, to the upland areas with a low population density. Such services as terrestial television, electricity, land-telephones all arrived late and required some financial support. There is no major hospital in the area. Mains gas is confined to the towns and one or two of the larger villages. Broadband for computers was available from 2005 and 'Freeserve' for multi-channel TV arrived in November 2009.

However, there are some services that have little purpose in urban areas but appear within extensive rural areas. Powys has eight Royal Mail bus services but London has none. They are Builth Wells to Abergwesyn (Brecon), Llandrindod to Llaithddu and Llandrindod to Rhayader (Radnor) and the following five in Mongomershire: Llanidloes to Dylife, Llanidloes to Llangurig, Machynlleth to Aberhosan, Newtown to New Mills and finally Welshpool to Y Foel.

The first experimental mail bus commenced between Llanidloes and Llangurig during February 1967. It was based at Llanidloes General Post Office under the supervision of the Newtown Postmaster. At this stage the GPO included telephones and must have had one of the largest commercial fleets in the UK. It acquired a 15 cwt van/minibus modified for passengers as well as a compartment for mail. The full timetable was not available until after the experimental period. Already Scotland and Northern Ireland had several bus services under contract to carry mail but the Llangurig bus was the first owned by the GPO. Ivor Parish of Morda recalls the purchase of an ex-MacBraynes Post Bus. It was a Bedford Super Vista short wheelbase vehicle on a heavy-duty chassis to withstand the poorer roads of the Highlands and Islands (*see Gittins of Dolanog for lighter chassis type, Chapter Six.*)

An investigation for a rural service took place in 1964 when the Ministry of Transport conducted an experiment between Dolanog and Welshpool (*see Llanfair section under Geraint Gittins, Chapter Six*) plus several others in England and Scotland. The Welshpool service was withdrawn after three months for want of passengers. Another company took on the closed MWM route between Y Foel and Welshpool but took it off within the year because it was not viable. The Ministry also considered allowing school buses to take stage fares but decided that this dual role had problems. (Many Powys stage routes currently combine school and stage fare but have the problem of no Saturday or holiday weeks service.) A further suggestion was that motorists could give lifts on an official basis but motorists would be reluctant to tie themselves to a timetable and there would be problems with insurance and liability compared with a common carrier. These were considered within the Jack Report of 1961. Rural access continued to be a concern for all including the politicians especially within the premise of never upsetting the Women's Institutes. The mail bus suggestion was pushed as a solution by then Minister of Transport. The one

The Royal Mail Peugot Partner bus parked at the Dylife letterbox at 4.01 pm. Postman Kevin Jones collects the posted letters. The afternoon circular loop will pass the Clywedog reservoir a little later. There would have been much industrial activity here in the 1870s from the lead mines with a township, church and school instead of a few farms and houses as now. Spoil can be observed behind the postbus. *Author (2005)*

The Royal Mail Renault Kangoo postbus works a long rural route from Llanidloes to Llangurig and Tylwch areas. Chris Norman collects mail and also shelters from the rain soon to turn to a cloudburst at Llidiart-y-waen school (1872 to 1969). The high moorlands suffered depopulation with the mechanization of farming and forestry. Such isolated all-age schools had no viable future once Llanidloes High School took all 11 plus age children. It was this that has led to the school contracts of feeder minbuses and coaches throughout the county. *Author (2005)*

experimental bus became permanent and now the County has eight such services and there are many others in the rural UK.

A general pattern of services can be discerned. The full timetables are held at the respective post offices and are published within the Powys Travel Guide. All services have the symbol of a kite indicating County Council financial support. The morning service leaves the local town at around 7.30 am and will take up to four hours to get to the furthest point as this bus is also the delivery van for every farm and house. The bus then returns along a more direct route and it is convenient for some passengers who wish to spend four hours in town. The afternoon routes proceed on a long loop. The other section of the loop is covered by a van only in the morning. This afternoon route stops at all the post boxes usually placed into a wall as any circular pillar-boxes are rare out of town. There are also several sub post offices/general stores on some routes. The bus leaves the local town close to 3.30 pm and will be back by 6.00 pm to connect with the SY (Shrewsbury) large van. Most services operate Mondays to Fridays only.

The postman starts a shift around 5.30 am to finish around 1.00 pm. The morning shift is usually allocated to the regular driver but the afternoon route is usually shared on an overtime basis. Passengers are issued with a card. The driver/postman then applies stamps with the value of the journey to the card and a ticket receipt is issued. Currently the routes with few passengers use a Renault Kangoo van with space for three passengers. The Newtown and Welshool routes go to several substantial villages and also serve several caravan

A Leyland DAF postbus collects a passenger outside Llanfair Caereinion Post Office/ General Stores in the early 1990s on the Welshpool to Y Foel service.

Powys County Council, Transport Co-ordination Unit

parks and outdoor leisure centres. These routes currently use an LDV van with eight seats. A security box and stacking shelves for parcels occupy the remaining space that would have four seats in a standard minibus. These vehicles will often be seen in the local town between lunch and afternoon departure on other mail duties.

The author travelled with postman Mark Tarrington on Thursday 14th July, 2005. The morning driver is Frank Roberts and Mark is one of six that share the afternoon rota. The bus collected three passengers at Newtown, two for Tregynon and one for Manafon. It would be rare not to have any passengers. The summary of the route is as follows. Newtown departure at 4.00 pm, Llanllwchaiarn 4.15, Bettws Cedewain 4.25, Tregynon 4.45, Manafon/New Mills 4.50, Llanwyddelan 4.55, Adfa 5.00, Cefn Coch 5.05, Waen-y-pant 5.15, Bwlch-y-ffridd 5.20, Aberhafesb 5.25 and Newtown completion at 5.37 pm. The stops are at letterboxes that are also empied in the morning. Some had only a few letters but substantial franked mail was collected at the University of Wales Centre at Gregynog. Parcels and special delivery envelopes were waiting for collection at Tregynon Post Office. It was a lovely experience being driven around the isolated communities. Sadly Post Bus services ceased in 2009.

Postman Mark Tarrington prepares to open the letterbox set in the wall of a private house at Bwlch-y-ffridd on the Newtown, New Mills afternoon circular. He would not wear such shorts in the winter for the bus has just descended into the shelter of the valley after crossing the high moorland below Mynydd Clogau. *Author (2005)*

Chapter Thirteen

The Stage Express Routes

Express routes have always been limited because of the nature of the roads and there being no large towns in the county. A vistor may see a goshawk at express speed leaving a conifer wood but will never see an Airport Express. The main historic express from within an independent was the Newtown to Cardiff route. Mid-Wales Motorways began this duty in 1953 on a daily basis. The coach left Newtown at 7.45 am and arrived in Cardiff at 12.40 taking five hours for a total of 110 miles. There was a connection at Builth with Knills (now Crossgates) for Knighton and Llandrindod. Crosville were soon to work this route from their depot at Llandrindod until depot closure in 1954. The coach left Cardiff at 5.30 pm and arrived at Newtown at 10.25 pm. There was a different pattern of service for Saturdays and Sundays. The service soon altered to daily only from July to September and operated on Mondays, Fridays and Saturdays for the other months. The Daimler coach was used for this run. A Crossley was also maintained to the standard for this elite route and supplements (two coaches) were necessary on occasions.

The service transferred to Crosville in late 1963 as the reformed Mid-Wales Motorways 1963 Ltd. gave up many routes and the home base now became Llanidloes. The Cardiff coach was withdrawn as Crosville struggled to make sense of the Newtown to Brecon rail replacement service. Crosville started an express to Liverpool every Thursday and to Manchester every Saturday. MWM attempted a Newtown to Birmingham service daily with an onward London connection from Digbeth (Birmingham bus station). Crosville added an express to Birmingham on Fridays from Llanidloes.

The Welsh Office created around 1966 gave support to a new concept that acquired the brand name of TrawsCambria (across Wales). Newtown bus station became the centre for exchange of two routes. These were Bangor to Cheltenham and Liverpool to Cardiff and these operated from the late 1960s and through the 70s until the closure of Cheltenham as a major hub for coach exchange.

Much of what follows is well documented elsewhere so only an incomplete summary is given. The National Bus Company was created and it was decided that all the bus companies with long distance coach services would market under a single brand. The National Express brand was the result and was under way by 1974. Some of the less important routes using smaller coaches remained with the provincial company.

Deregulation led to the private National Express and several competitors. National Express Holdings was to own Crosville Cymru during a very troubled short period in the late 1980s. The system evolved to that of franchise. Mid Wales Travel had the franchise for one bus to work from Shrewsbury to Leeds in the 1980s. The Liverpool-Cardiff route via Newtown struggled on with Crosville Cymru and National Welsh of Cardiff. The latter company went bankrupt with no notice in 1991 much to the embarrassment of the politicians and owners. The

Telephone :
Newtown 345

Telegrams :
Mid-Wales Motorways Newtown

Mid-Wales Motorways Limited

(*Reg. Office* : **Transport House, Severn Square, Newtown, Mid-Wales)**

PASSENGER ROAD TRANSPORT OPERATORS

EXPLORE THE UNRIVALLED BEAUTIES OF CENTRAL WALES
"POWYSLAND—THE PARADISE OF WALES"
THE MID-WALES MOTORWAY'S WAY

LUXURY COACHES ARE AT YOUR SERVICE AND PRIVATE PARTIES ESPECIALLY CATERED FOR

OUR PUBLIC SERVICES ALSO OPERATE THROUGHOUT CENTRAL WALES AND INTO SHROPSHIRE AND AN EXPRESS COACH SERVICE DAILY (RETURN) BETWEEN NEWTOWN AND CARDIFF VIA LLANIDLOES, RHAYADER, BUILTH, BRECON, MERTHYR TYDFIL AND PONTYPRIDD

Enquiries invited of our Reg. Office

Postcard publicity for MWM details the daily express service including Sundays. Economics soon dictated that the winter service was three days per week (Monday, Friday and Saturday) and daily services only operated in summer. *John Griffiths, Aberhafesb*

The Daimler BEP 252 was purchased for the Cardiff/Newtown express. The coach is seen parked at Cardiff bus station in the mid-1950s. *David Hughes, Shrewsbury*

The Mid Wales Travel Volvo B58 moves out of Barker Street on the journey to Leeds within the franchise of National Express. David was to drive the Midland Red bus to Oswestry. He has a clear event of that day because a car being driven at excess speed lost control and hit the bus close to Oswestry. It was a miracle that the young driver survived his stupidity. The police estimated impact speed at 60 mph as the bus had already stopped. *David Hughes, Shrewsbury*

The National Express pick-up point is at the information centre at Welshpool. The coach is parked 400 yards from the main bus stop but it has a clear route both off and return to the bypass so that time can be maintained. The Scania Van Hool T9 Alizée is owned by the Birmingham Coach Company. Note the frequency of photographs within the towns where a car has parked on double yellow lines with no thought of any larger vehicles. *Author (2005)*

Development Board for Rural Wales
Timetable 1979. Guide only.
National Express Routes

X4 Aberystwyth to Chester. Th & Sat. May to Sept. Machynlleth, Newtown, Welshpool, Llanymynech.
X5 Aberystwyth to Liverpool, Sat only, May to Sept. Machynlleth.
X6 Aberystwyth to Birmingham, Sat. Machynlleth, Newtown, Welshpool.
X7 Aberystwyth to Ross on Wye, Mon to Sat, May to Sept. Llangurig.
X10 Bangor to Cheltenham, Daily including Sunday, May to Sept. Machynlleth, Newtown, Churchstoke.
X12 Barmouth to Leamington Spa. Sat. May to Sept. Llanfair and Welshpool
X13 Barry Island via Cardiff to Liverpool. Daily, May to Sept. Llangurig, Llanidloes, Newtown, Welshpool, Llanymynech.
X16 Haverfordwest to Liverpool. Sat. May to Sept. Newtown only for break.
X20 Pwllheli to London, Friday only. Llanfair, Welshpool.

Most stop at Newtown for ¾ hr for toilet, refreshments and exchange.

Red Kite Coaches of Aberystwyth introduced a Thursday and Saturday express to Manchester in February 2005. Paul Bryan brings the Daf Van Hool into the Newtown bus station at 9.07 am.
Author (2005)

result was that coaches from both Rhondda Bus and Dinas Caerdydd were seen in Newtown until the service ceased.

TrawsCambria was rebuilt as a new route from Holyhead to Bristol via Bangor, Machynlleth, Aberystwyth, Carmarthen, Swansea, Cardiff and Newport. This connected a series of towns including Lampeter that all have higher education centres with potential for student carriage. It was reduced to Bangor to Cardiff and ceased in 2004. Currently Arriva Cymru work a limited stop bus from Bangor to Aberystwyth and First Cymru work from Aberystwyth to Carmarthen with only two connections on to Cardiff. The journey takes 8 hours compared with Bangor to Cardiff by train via Chester and Crewe taking between 4½ and 5 hours. Communications between North and South Wales has always been a matter of political concern and the need to travel has grown with the role of Cardiff within devolution.

It is known that the Welsh Assembly is looking with some concern at the problem and certain express routes may be reinstated or improved in the future. A limited air route from Valley (Anglesey) to Cardiff Rhoose is also under consideration but this will not help Montgomeryshire unless Welshpool airport has an upgrading for such services. Any solution is dependent on substantial subsidy.

National Express only operates one through route through Montgomeryshire in 2009. This is the daily (including Sunday) Aberystwyth to London service. It is routed through Ponterwyd, Llangurig and Llanidloes while the train travels via Machynlleth. The journey to London takes about twice the time of the train. The franchise is with the Birmingham Coach Company. It picks up in Newtown at 09.35 hrs and the London return arrives at Newtown bus station at 18.50 hrs.

Several other stage routes operate on certain days. Red Kite of Aberystwyth runs a Thursday and Saturday service to Manchester. Lloyds of Machynlleth runs a Chester services on the first and third Saturday of each month. Red Dragon Group Travel (ex-Beadles of Newtown) runs a coach between school contracts. The Shrewsbury Whizzer operates every Wednesday, The Wrexham Winner runs on the second and fourth Monday of each month and the Aberystwyth Arrow is a Thursday service in the summer only. Tanat Valley Express Services operate in summer only to Aberyswyth (Fridays), Llandudno (Mondays) and Blackpool (Saturdays).

The Welsh Assembly have plans to enhance the TrawsCambria with improvements along the western route and to reintroduce a Newtown/Brecon/Methyr route timed in with rail and other coach services. This is the old Mid-Wales Railway route from which Crosville withdrew the rail replacement service in the mid-1960s. It follows the attempted Newtown to Cardiff route pioneered by MWM in 1953.

Crosville Leyland 112 parked at Llangurig village centre. It is thought to be on the short-lived Rhayader/Llanidloes/ Newtown route in late 1924. Crosville had moved this bus from the tram connection at Huyton in Liverpool. If a bus had a soul, it must have found the contrast from an urban service to this isolated route in the Cambrian Mountains immense. *Mrs Ann Addison, Llangurig*

Tom Higgs's writing is on the reverse: 'Leyland 32 seater 1926 at garage at Trewythen Hotel'. The date of 1926 is significant. Crosville had a depot at Trewythen, Llanidloes in 1924 but then moved to Llandrindod Wells within a few months. The coaching inn at Trewythen became the parking area for Crosville and this bus would have received full service or any repair from the Aberystwyth depot. *The Higgs family, Llanidloes*

Chapter Fourteen

Crosville and succession

The Crosville story is well documented in many other volumes. The percentage of business turnover in Montgomeryshire must have been imperceptible compared with routes in the Wirral between Chester and Birkenhead. Books on Crosville history therefore often only have a small reference to Montgomeryshire operations and local photography is not common. This chapter will therefore look at local recall from the Llanidloes sub-depot and from several men who transferred from Mid-Wales Motorways to Crosville.

A very brief outline of Crosville follows. The name of the company is derived from Crosland Taylor and George de Ville in a partnership that set out to assemble and sell a French car design based from a warehouse in Chester in 1905. The first bus service was between Chester and Ellesmere Port prior to World War I. The company expanded by new routes and take-overs from a base in Chester and then moved along the North Wales Coast and then down the Cambrian coast to Aberystwyth and beyond.

The Llanidloes and Llandrindod development is covered in the recall of the Higgs family. The GWR and Corris Railway companies had developed feeder services including buses based at Machynlleth and Welshpool.

This section merged with Wrexham Tramways to form Western Transport that traded for around two years. Ivor Parish of Morda has documentation where his father signed an agreement with Western Transport to feed into Llanymynech and various points on the Llanfair to Oswestry bus route. The company merged with Crosville in 1934. This is the reason why Oswestry (Western Transport) depot was always considerd part of Crosville in Wales.

The company was within the influence of BET in the 1930s but became part of the Tilling Group in 1942. Crosville and the Tilling Group became part of the British Transport Commission with ease as many Crosville shares were held by the GWR and London Midland & Scottish Railway (LMS). Also the Tilling Group negotiated the retention of their company brand names and local autonomy. Crosland Taylor had a major role assisting all bus companies and Parliament with legislation in the 1930s; he would now be called a consultant.

The company expanded in Montgomeryshire after World War II with rail closures taking on the Llangynog route (1951) and Welshpool to Oswestry (1965). The replacement Newtown to Brecon Service (1963) only lasted a few years before being withdrawn. MWM's trading difficulties led to transfer of express services around 1963 and the acquisition of the Newtown to Shrewsbury service that was soon rationalized to a Llanidloes to Shrewsbury route. All companies, including the independents, started to face problems from 1950 onwards. Wages and fuel costs rose and the customer base fell due to private car use. Barbara Castle, the then Minister of Transport, set legislation to form the National Bus Company with the 1968 Transport Act. The problem of rural bus support was defined within social need and local government help.

Guide to Crosville Motor Services in Montgomeryshire and borders

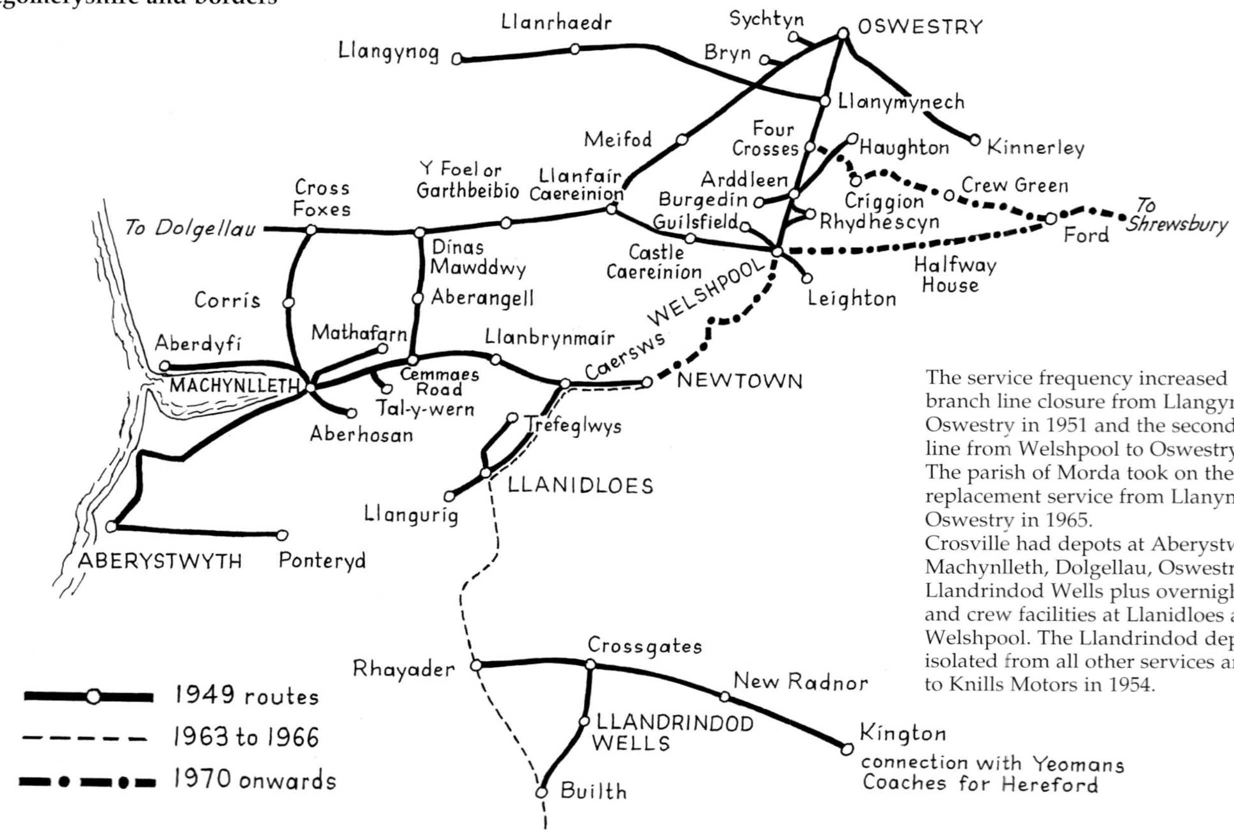

The service frequency increased with the branch line closure from Llangynog to Oswestry in 1951 and the secondary main line from Welshpool to Oswestry in 1965. The parish of Morda took on the rail replacement service from Llanymynech to Oswestry in 1965.

Crosville had depots at Aberystwyth, Machynlleth, Dolgellau, Oswestry and Llandrindod Wells plus overnight parking and crew facilities at Llanidloes and Welshpool. The Llandrindod depot was isolated from all other services and passed to Knills Motors in 1954.

Route maps Montgomeryshire/Powys Autumn 2005

Post Bus Services

- A. Llandrindond-Llaithddu
- B. Llanidloes-Dylife
- C. Llanidloes-Llangurig-Tyfwch
- D. Machynlleth-Aberhosan
- E. Newtown-New Mills
- F. Welshpool-Y Foel

Market Day-Only Services

- G. Browns: Builth-Newtown (Tuesdays)
- H. Owens: Knighton-Newtown (Tuesdays)
- I. Whittles: Ludlow-Clun-Newtown (Tuesdays)
- J. Whittle: Bishops Castle-Welshpool (Mondays)
- K. Minsterley Motors: Pontesbury-Newtown (Tuesdays)
- L. Boultons: Churchstoke-Shrewsbury (Wednesdays)
- M. Mid-Wales: Llanfair-Newtown (Tuesdays)
- N. Parish: Pontrobert-Oswestry (Wednesdays)
- O. Tanat Valley: Llansilin-Oswestry (Wednesdays)
- P. Lloyds: Dinas Mawddy-Machynlleth (service supplemented on Wednesdays - market day)

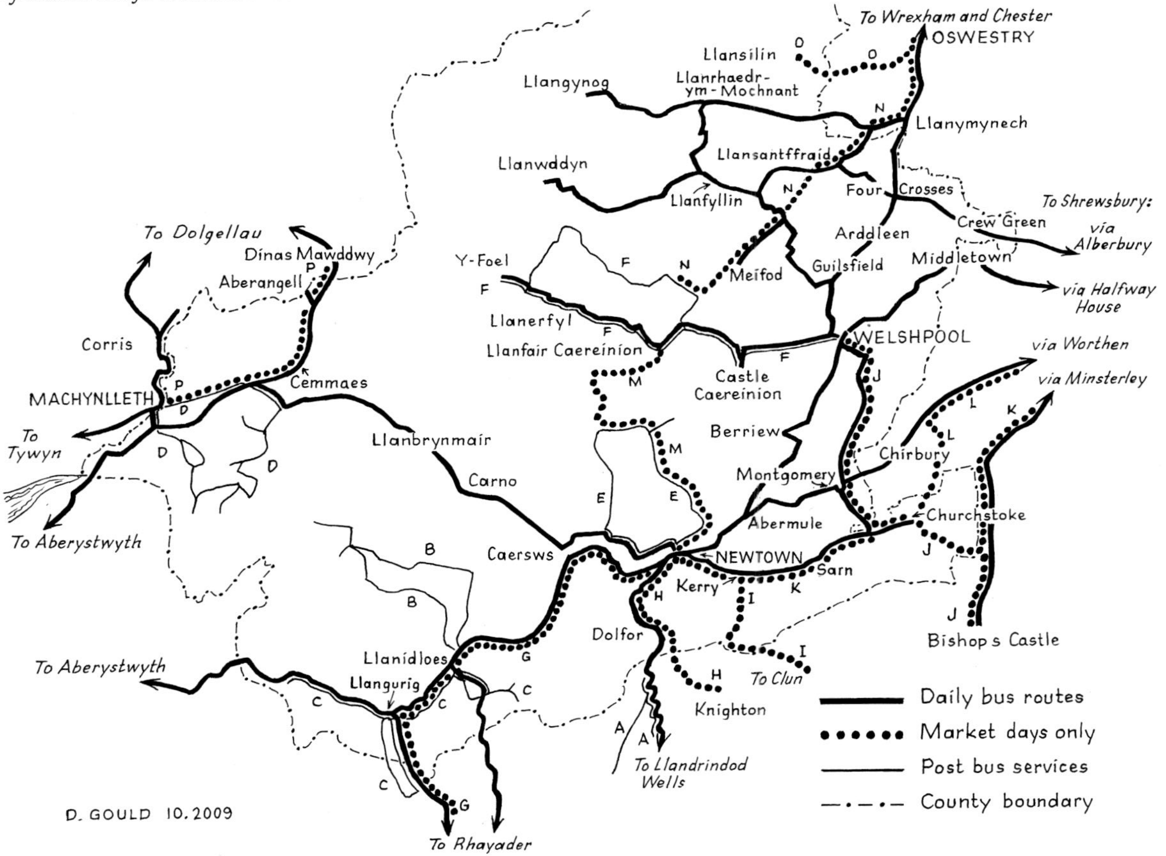

To Wrexham and Chester
OSWESTRY
Llansilin
Llangynog
Llanrhaedr-ym-Mochnant
Llanymynech
Llansantffraid
Llanwddyn
Llanfyllin
Four Crosses
To Shrewsbury:
Crew Green
via Alberbury
Arddleen
Middletown
via Halfway House
Guilsfield
Meifod
Y-Foel
Llanerfyl
Llanfair Caereinion
WELSHPOOL
via Worthen
via Minsterley
Castle Caereinion
Berriew
Chirbury
Montgomery
Churchstoke
Abermule
NEWTOWN
Sarn
Kerry
Bishop s Castle
Dolfor
To Clun
Knighton
To Llandrindod Wells
To Dolgellau
Dinas Mawddwy
Aberangell
Corris
Cemmaes
MACHYNLLETH
To Tywyn
To Aberystwyth
Llanbrynmair
Carno
Caersws
Llanidloes
Llangurig
To Aberystwyth
To Rhayader
D. GOULD 10.2009

Daily bus routes
Market days only
Post bus services
County boundary

Above left: Tom arrives for his shift at Trewythen in 1926. He would have travelled from Llandinam. Tom's writing on the reverse: 'Truimph 4½hp 1920 model with belt drive' and then becomes too faded to read. *The Higgs family, Llanidloes*

Above right: Several Bristol MW6G units were held in Mid-Wales for the long-distance stage routes. In 1964, Tom, recently retired, stands with a Crosville lady, maybe the wife of an Aberystwyth driver. Note the shelter and part of the Crosville office that stood at Y Gro until demolished in the late 1980s. *The Higgs family, Llanidloes*

Colin Higgs, on the left and his friend, Terry Walden, stand in front of the Crosville coach at Harlescott (Shrewsbury). Dad was the driver and they were on their way to the very popular Hawkstone motorcycle scramble event. The Brisol KW was the pioneer coach with full cab in the early 1950s. These were allocated to the Liverpool-London express route. Colin dates the picture to around 1958 so one of the Bristol KWs had been cascaded down to Llanidloes.

The Higgs family, Llanidloes

The bus companies may well have become overdependent on subsidy income and lost some ability to innovate.

What follows next is still a debate of wisdom or stupidity. The Transport Act of 1985 brought forward deregulation and privatization. Nicholas Ridley, the then Minister of Transport, split Crosville into a Welsh and an English section against consultant advice. It placed the Crosville Welsh section in immediate difficulty. Various companies held the portfolio. The name of Crosville Cymru (Wales) evolved with a very colourful livery compared with the previous Crosville green. A Crosville management ownership just did not have enough capital so it moved in succession to National Express and then Amberline of Liverpool and then with a group of investors associated with Drawlane Transport of Salisbury. Property dispersal may or may not have been necessary but the accusation of asset stripping came to be prevalent. The company moved to a holding company called British Bus. The Chairman made a desperate attempt to relieve financial pressure and the accounting procedures led to him receiving a prison sentence. The company was hours from receivership on several occasions and was valued at £1 with liabilities and assets. In South Wales, the National Welsh Company collapsed into chaos. Crosville had acquired much goodwill from 1920s to the 1980s in North Wales.

The political structure had given a Conservative Government for the UK with little support in Wales that finally culminated in no Welsh Conservative MPs for a decade. The perception was that of private greed having removed well-respected companies and good jobs. The debate of how to run a bus company for the community continues and there may not be a correct solution. Anyhow the Cowie Group based in Sunderland had aquired professional skill in bus management and was acquiring companies including Crosville and Midland Red. In 1967, they decided on the brand name of Arriva and this takes the story to the present day. The successions of changes in the late 1980s left staff and passengers bewildered and maybe a better word would be traumatized. Much business including most school contracts, private hire and excursion and some stage routes were lost to the independents. So again, the question must be asked. Was the period of 1985 to around 1993 one of wisdom or one of stupidity?

Crosville and Llanidloes

Tom Higgs started to work for Crosville in 1924. Tom was born in 1898 on a farm in the upper area of the Van and part of the holding is now under the Clywedog reservoir. Tom served in World War I and was wounded. He was discharged after hospital treatment. He needed lighter duties than a return to the family farm so he took on duties as a taxi driver for a local Llanidloes garage. He started to drive lorries and then became a bus driver for Evans Motors of Aberystwyth for three years. He took the opportunity to join Crosville when they opened a bus station at Llanidloes in 1924. The bus station lasted less than a year and moved to Llandrindod Wells until closure in 1954.

This information was given by two of the children: Colin, the youngest born in 1944 and Hazel the oldest born in 1927. Tom lived on to the age of nearly 103.

Tom's writing: 'Approaching Rhallt lane, 1926, Leyland Lion Half Cab 36 seater'. The service would have been the daily Llanidloes to Newtown route that commenced on 8th October, 1924.

The Higgs family, Llanidloes

The photograph shows wear but the faces remain clear. The reverse has 1958, Llanidloes depot, Crosville. Verdun Higgs (son) recalls the staff *from left to right*: Tom Higgs with plaque for safe driving, R. Brunt, H. Bound, Mair Remsbottom, S. Remsbottom, J. Morgan, George Jones and Bill Evans. Mair was the clerical officer and both she and her husband moved to Chester Head Office when one of them received promotion. All the others were the local drivers.

The Higgs family, Llanidloes

Both children thought it was a shame that the interviews could not have taken place around 2001 as Dad was lucid until the final few months and much valued information departed with him.

The main Crosville service was that from Llanidloes to Newtown and the buses were serviced for decades from Aberystwyth depot. Dad was sometimes sent to Llandrindod but disliked this duty as he had to stop in lodgings. The isolated Llandrindod depot had a service between Kington, Llandrindod and Builth.

Hazel recalls that the family lived at Llandinam until around 1936 so Dad had a series of motorbikes to travel to Llanidloes daily as well as stopping in lodgings. The main duty became Newtown to Llanidloes. There were extra duties in World War II including a works service to the government shadow factory of Accles and Pollock (Birmingham) at Newtown. Many ladies were employed to build machined parts for aircraft. There was also movement of Italian prisoners of war to forest sites. Another duty took place in the late 1940s. British Railways renewed much of their track locally. This work was done on Sundays and would have included any section of the Cambrian track. The Llanidloes and Caersws staff was used on a voluntary overtime basis and the bus could travel down to Brecon or out to Oswestry or up the Coast Line. Tom retired in 1964 after 40 years with Crosville. He always tried to remain on his regular route as the long distance routes developed to Cardiff, Liverpool etc. Younger men such as George Jones took on such duties. Hazel recorded that the last bus from Newtown arrived at Llanidloes at 11.50 pm and would be packed on Friday and Saturday evenings. The driver and the conductor had to refuel and clean the bus at the end of the shift. This meant that Dad would not be back in the house on that shift till nearly 1.00 am. Dad also helped Trevor Jones (*see Celtic Travel, Chapter Four*) on the Saturday Llangurig Llanidloes bus after he retired for a few years. He became a well-known character after retirement with his beloved pushbike. Colin still has the bike in the garden and he hopes to restore it as a memento for Tom Higgs, 1898 to 2002.

George Jones or George Crosville or Jones y bws

George was born in the locality at Llawryglyn in 1915 and the family moved to Y Fan soon afterwards. George was the youngest of a large family. Sadly both parents died when he was a young child and one of the older sisters gave up her work to look after them. It was a tough childhood heavily dependent on charity. George left school at 14 to work on a local farm. He took the opportunity for greater independence and more money to work for a contract when an underground cable for the GPO telephones was laid from Newtown to Aberystwyth. He would cycle every day to work. There was no mechanization, the whole trench and backfill was done by hand. He commenced work in the forests around 1939 cutting out thinnings for pit props and found that he was in a reserved occupation. He drove a local van for delivery after World War II until joining Crosville in the mid-1950s.

He started as a conductor. One of the drivers would be Tom Higgs. Tom lived to 102 and became one of the characters of Llanidloes during his long retirement as he toured the roads on his bicycle. He once went down a street that had just become one way and the local policeman advised him; ' Tom, it is a one way street now' and the reply came, 'But I am only going one way'. He was a most honest man and a joy to know.

The buses started to convert to one-man-operation and George took his PSV test in the late 1950s. One double-deck, three single-deck buses and one coach were kept out in the open at Y Gro. They were all Bristols as far as George can remember. The half-cabs had an entrance at the rear for passengers to board and the conductor to stand but they were soon to be replaced by buses for one-man-operation. There were two small offices that were built just after World War II. One was the mess rooom with space to collate the takings and the other was a small office for the supervisor and customer contact. There was a staff toilet, a diesel tank and a lockup lean-to for the cleaning equipment. It was basic and must have been all knocked down by the mid-1980s. The buses were serviced at the Aberystwyth depot. This was a good roster for the bus would be driven to the depot. This took an hour and then there was five hours free time before coming home unless a bus was switched. There was no direct stage route from Aberystwyth to Llanidloes for much of this period. The wage slips came from the Oswestry depot and full staff records such as pensions were kept at Chester. The Llanidloes workers were members of the Oswestry club but this was too far away ever to consider.

A major change took place when the former Mid-Wales Railway closed in December 1962. The rail replacement service ran from Newtown station to Brecon via Llanidloes, Rhayader and Builth. The idea was to connect with buses at Brecon with connections for Newport, Hereford, Methyr/Cardiff and Swansea. The service ran for about three years only. Few rail customers transferred to the bus so it was very lightly-loaded and obviously would not be viable once the interim railway support ceased. It was a delight to drive on the route. The next and major change occurred in February 1970 when Mid-Wales Motorways surrendered its Newtown-Shrewsbury route. Crosville took this on and immediately made Llanidloes to Shrewsbury a continuous route.

One Llanidloes bus was timed to arrive at Newtown for the TrawsCambria interchange when the Cheltenham-Bangor and the Liverpool-Cardiff coaches crossed. George has taken the TrawsCambria several times to Cardiff or Liverpool for sickness or holiday cover. Crosville would also ask him to help at the Machynlleth depot so he has worked buses to Tywyn, Aberystwyth, Corris, Dolgellau, etc.

The buses could be packed with people standing in the 1950s. The car relentlessly poached bus passengers. Someone would thank George for his help but the person had just passed the driving test and had purchased a second-hand car and would also take his/her friend to work. The car also slowed the bus progress with congestion. Often the service would only have a few passengers by the 1970s and late evening services were cut back.

Llanidloes is in the shadow of the Cambrian Mountains and can receive very heavy rain and strong wind. George had collected four girls at Wolverhampton who wished to camp in Wales. The Birmingham coach arrived at Llanidloes in the late evening with the rain smashing against the windows. George suggested that their mission was impossible at that moment and suggested that they stay in the coach and keep everything tidy. They had left by the time he returned in the morning but had left a note thanking him and suggested that God had sent him. He arrived another evening with similar weather conditions and a young lady was obviously perturbed. She was trying to get to Dolgellau and should have been on the Machynlleth bus. George took her home and Mrs Jones prepared a warm meal. The young girl was soon fast asleep in a warm bed. George made contact with her parents who collected her the following day. The Jones continued to receive a Christmas card greeting for many a year from that grateful teenager. Such acts of kindness are almost certainly still done by those who work in the bus industry.

Gareth Jones (son of George Jones)

Gareth joined Crosville in 1979 when it was still part of the National Bus Company and dad was soon to retire. Gareth had been a HGV driver for Aber Carriers of Welshpool before that date. He had to take a PSV test. Crosville arranged this within the busy traffic of Chester with a double-deck bus. The test took four hours. Gareth recalls that the examiner had a suction pad with a measuring pole that was placed on both sides of the bus and the vehicle had to be at least one foot from the kerb when reversed.

Four buses were kept at the Welshpool sub-depot and serviced from Oswestry. Many changes were to follow from de-regulation and privatization. Both Welshpool and Llanidloes depots closed and the Abermule depot was created; buses were serviced at Aberystwyth. Midland Red took over the Oswestry depot and buses changed to Midland Red stock from Shrewsbury. Nick Culliford made a bid for school contracts of Powys County Council from the Oswestry depot in the final year of operation as Crosville Cymru. The contract was awarded and there was an immediate problem of not enough buses so many older buses were transferred from Wrexham and elsewhere. Ken Jones became a full-time fitter at Abermule and buses also had to be parked overnight at the Welshpool and Newtown public car parks. The contract could only have lasted a year. The buses were only for school contract and the independents made sure they retained mid-day business and all the local excursion work. They got most of their school contract work back.

Gareth worked mainly on stage work from Shrewsbury to Llanidloes and the Newtown town service. He was once asked to collect a group of American tourists from a broken-down luxury coach near Welshpool. They had to spend the remainder of the day in a stage bus to Llangollen, the Horse Shoe Pass and Chester. They were grateful that the problem for the day was solved. The late John Emberton looked after the Llanfair Caereinion to Welshpool route with a morning and afternoon service using a small Bristol bus. This service finished in the early 1990s leaving the town with only a Royal Mail bus for a few years. Gareth thought that the Llanfair-Oswestry service finished about the same time that he joined in 1979.

Arriva Midlands North finally had some quality control after a decade of chaos. The buses were based at Abermule. There was a portacabin with toilets, mess room, washing facilities etc. with an adjoining shed with oil and cleaning fluids; the yard has floodlights. Each bus was allocated time every other day to call at Shrewbury depot for topping up with diesel fuel. A cleaner would valet

Right: Gareth Jones sits at the wheel of a bus during the Midland Red period in the early 1990s. Passengers have praised Gareth and his courtesy and several have written poems in praise of him. *George Jones, Llanidloes*

Below: George Jones has a staff pass from Arriva. George, at 92 years of age, is unlikely to make great use of this concession but he assumes he could get free travel on any Arriva company including a trip around a Dutch or Italian suburb. The concession is inherited from Crosville.
George Jones, Llanidloes

Gareth Jones (*left*) having retired from Crosville/Arriva driver continues part-time driving helping Geoff Hancock (right) of Rhiew Valley Motors, Berriew. Hancocks have the school contract for Welshpool High School from Middletown, Guilsfield via Groes and Guilsfield via Penrhos plus excursion and leisure trips. Rhiew Valley Motors was the name choosen by Ned 'Grocer' Evans in the 1920s prior to joining MWM in 1937. *Author (2005)*

the inside of the bus and the outside was placed through a wash as the driver was allocated an hour break. The five to six men at Abermule worked on four daily shifts on a rota basis. The first shift reported at 05.15 and finished at 15.40. The final shift started at 11.44 and finished at 19.20. This still leaves one problem of no late services or Sunday services and George supposes they would be provided if there were enough customers. The men work a five-day week with the rest day moving in sequence from Monday to Saturday. Any driver would be asked to work a rest day for sickness cover. There was a far larger pool of drivers at Shrewsbury and they could also take on relief duty.

Gareth recalls some details of the problems of the changes of post-privatization. The first error was to split Crosville Wales and Crosville England by the order of Nicholas Ridley. Most senior staff with technical understanding opted for the larger English company. It was the poor driver who had to face discontent from passengers. Gareth is one of many that have little but contempt for these aspects of Margaret Thatcher and her premiership. The company was purchased at a discount and the more modern buses were sold off and replaced by older units. Then depots were sold off or leased for development so staff would have to try to present clean buses from derelict sites. The customer base declined.

Gareth would not classify himself as an economist but he certainly understands the meaning of asset stripping through practical experience. The Arriva Company stabilized the situation with professional bus management skills. Gareth worked the final 10 years within a skilled bus company after a decade of problems. Gareth retired at 65 years of age in 2004. He drives the school contract for Rhiew Valley Motors from Middletown to Welshpool High School and will help the owner, Geoff Hancock, with any standby duties. The National Bus Company pension rights were taken to the European Court and have been protected. Gareth has a good pension but the younger men coming through the system of any company may well struggle to have such a good deal.

A bus driver faces many facets of the public during the day. Most are very good and it is pleasant to help anyone who appreciates the service. The work is not without amusing experiences. Left luggage must occur virtually every day. A packet of sweets or a newspaper makes little difference but often a carrier bag would not only contain shopping but a purse full of credit cards etc. Teeth, glasses, hats and walking sticks have all been found. A prescription medicine was always a cause of concern to the person who had mislaid such an item. Gareth was once drawing out of Shrewsbury bus station when he saw a lady in the wing mirror. She was waving frantically because she had left her baby on the bus! Gareth was glad that he noticed her because he would have been uncertain what to do if he had taken the baby to Llanidloes.

John James Crosville

Advice was given to find John. It would be typical of a Welsh rural area that the name given was John Bryn Gwalia or John Crosville. John had ceased living at the smallholding of Bryn Gwalia at Llangadfan 45 years ago and the name of Crosville ceased 15 years ago. John started his bus career with Mid-Wales

MWM Bedford OWB EP 8332 was registered with the company in November 1942. It is parked at Oswestry with Four Crosses as destination during World War II. Stage route access was only on Wednesday market day so this bus may have worked through earlier from the Welshpool or Halfway House depot. *Ewart Buxton, Ford near Shrewsbury*

Guy Arab VS 4353 ex-Western SMT worked the Montgomery to Shrewsbury service during the peak loading in the early 1950s. The closed rear door was an additional fitting. The photograph was taken in the then Worthen yard. A Dennis Lancet is under cover. *Ewart Buxton, Ford near Shrewsbury*

Motorways at the Llanfair depot. This was on the B4389 to Newtown just before the fierce gradient and the junction to Cefn Coch. It is currently owned by Wynnstay Farmers. The date would be around 1960 with only two more years of work from the depot. There was one Crossley half-cab and five to six Bedfords mainly OBs.

The main service was from Y Foel to Llanfair. The timetables gave the bus starting at Garthbeibio and that is the church and also the alternative name for Y Foel. Only the Monday service worked through to Welshpool. All others made a connection at Llanfair with the Crosville service. The service was already in decline and was down to two or three buses daily.

The Monday services to Welshpool consisted of one from Y Foel, one from Pontrobert both using the trunk road and one from Cefn Coch. The Cefn Coch bus meandered along the lanes via Adfa, New Mills and Manafon to Berriew and then along the main road. The Tuesday service to Newtown fair had two to three buses according to demand. The Wednesday service was a bus that left Y Foel via Llanfair and Meifod to Oswestry. Thursday had a monthly fair day service from Llanfair via Llwydiarth to Llanfyllin. Friday had the Llanfair extra in from the Foel and Saturday had one or two buses via Meiford to Four Crosses with a connection to Oswestry. The bus proceeded via Crewgreen to Shrewsbury. It was incredible that the older drivers can recall these buses full with standing passengers a decade earlier.

Vernon Evans ('Bus to Bosworth') had already moved to Newtown. The yard closed in 1963 so John moved to help Selwyn Hughes with a continuation of the Foel to Llanfair Service but it was to be of no avail. John returned to MWM around 1965 with the duty of driving the Newtown to Shrewsbury service from the depot at Welshpool. Vehicles used would have included the Sentinels. John transferred to Crosville when Mid-Wales surrendered the operating licence. The bus would usually be a Bristol RE single-decker. The story is then similar to Gareth moving from Crosville to Crosville Cymru to Midland Red to Arriva. The line manager for Powys was Wyn Lloyd (*see Lloyds Coaches, Machynlleth Chapter Five*) for several years and that young man had really grasped the knowledge of route management. The depot became Shrewsbury with the park at Abermule and most buses for the final year of John's work were variations of Volvo city buses. John had a health problem and was interviewed when on sick leave. He knew that he would have to retire just before reaching 65 years of age because his PSV licence would be revoked. John would act a relief driver for the TrawsCambria crossover at Newtown and would normally take the Bangor service (ex-Cheltenham) on to the north.

The depot at Welshpool

Ewart Buxton was born in 1930. His earliest transport memory was walking with his father watching horses tow the barges into the canal basin at Newtown in what was the twilight of commercial use. Ewart joined the army and learnt the trade of a vehicle fitter within the RAOC. He joined MWM in the early 1950s and was the fitter/driver at the Worthen depot. He would move to Newtown

Bristol VRT highbridge double-decker working the Newtown D81 town service close to the hospital on the Llanfair Road. The vehicle was one of several purchased for the school contract awarded for a short period in the early 1990s. The older bus had already worked for Sheffield Corporation and the South Yorkshire PTE. An Oswestry man came down to post new timetables at each bus stop. He borrowed one of these buses and made an error of jamming the roof under the Dolfor rail bridge. *Ewart Buxton, Ford near Shrewsbury*

Driver Gareth Jones struggles to clean a Leyland National at the Abermule depot. Conditions were not easy in many rented post-privatization yards. *Ewart Buxton, Ford near Shrewsbury*

for short periods for staff cover or a major workshop duty. Ewart transferred to Tom Green's company for a year when Tom purchased that section of the company. He returned to MWM in 1964 and David Pye took on his role at Worthen. Ewart's main duty was to be mechanic/driver at Welshpool. The first duty early in the morning was to check all vehicles including the Sentinels. He would then work the Leighton, Trelystan school bus and then take a bus to Newtown for service or take the school bus and assist in the Newtown yard prior to the afternoon school run.

Crosville (1970) and then the National Bus Company took on the Llanidloes to Shrewsbury route. The yard was shared with Mid-Wales (school buses) and Crosville. Ewart continued with Mid-Wales for a year. He qualified as a Goods Vehicle Inspector including PSVs but decided to use it as an in-house duty. He joined Crosville as one of a team of eight drivers at Welshpool. The main duty was the Llanidloes to Shrewsbury route including the extras that started from Welshpool for Shrewsbury. He would cover the Llanfair route when the late John Emberton was not available. The route to Oswestry would be another duty including the Monday and Wednesday extra that went to some of the smaller communities. The other route covered from Welshpool was Four Crosses to Shrewsbury via Crew Green. There were up to three per day all via Criggion. This route was to cease for several years until started again by Arriva Midlands North and now Tanat Valley Coaches.

Ewart started married life at Worthen. Margaret was a lass from Rorrington. She would have travelled to Marton Primary School in Bill Hailstone's Churchstoke bus. Crosville would also use Ewart on the Oswestry to Ellesmere run. Crosville took over Vaggs of Knockin at very short notice in 1982. Ewart was assigned the duty of disposal preparation of the older coaches. The depot transferred to Oswestry and use of Bristol and Leyland buses. This was covered within a period of weeks. Ewart continued on with Arriva after the age of 65 as a cover driver. He now lives at Ford with the bus stop to either Shrewsbury or Llanidloes almost outside his front door.

Much of the knowledge that Ewart discussed already has been described by others. Gareth Jones, John James and Ewart are the last that knew the operation of Crosville in the early 1970s. All recall the luxury of driving the heavy-bodied Seddon Pennine. One duty was to cut up the burnt frames ready to load for scrap after the Newtown yard fire in 1967. This would have included the three Sentinels. One of Ewart's friends was an apprentice with Sentinel and can recall a member of the Ricardo family sent from the Argentine to assist with the diesel engine design. The last steam lorries produced in the late 1940s were for an Argentinian order and it as thought that the diesel engine licence for manufacture may have been a reciprocal arrangement. Again Ewart recalls the astonishing standard of engineering of the Sentinels. It truly was a flawed beauty. Ewart has a considerable photographic record and several across a 55 year career in the bus industry are here included. There are also numerous illustrations of Crosville activity within the section on Lloyds Coaches and the photography of David Hughes.

A Midland Red Leyland National D71 prepares to leave Welshpool for Oswestry soon after the Oswestry depot transferred from Crosville Cymru to Midland Red after December 1991.
Ewart Buxton, Ford near Shrewsbury

The Arriva Cymru bus waits at Y Gro at Llanidloes prior to departure for Aberystwyth. The Crosville building would have stood near the shed behind. The service is one of the 'G' prefix funded by the Welsh Assembly and is shared between Arriva and Crossgates (working through from Llandrindod Wells). There are now five services daily. The names 'Y Gro' at Llanidloes and 'The Gravel' at Newtown are interchangeable as both refer to a stretch of the river where rate of flow deposits round small stones almost certainly going back to glacial melt. The technical term is river braiding.
Author (2005)

Arriva Midlands North service 75 from Llanidloes to Shrewsbury crosses the iron-arch bridge designed by Sweetman in 1872. The photograph has been taken from the base of the rail bridge and also shows the shorter grass caused by boot wear on the long distance Offa's Dyke footpath. The journey from Newtown to Shrewsbury takes 1 hour 20 minutes with 18 listed town and village stops. A bridge at this point near Buttington may go back as far as the 14th century or earlier and this may explain the Welsh name of Talybont. *Author (2005)*

The Machynlleth to Newtown Arrriva route 522 approaches Talerddig at 2.40 pm. The bridge carries the railway over the steep embankment that was cut and carried from the famous Talerddig cutting. Many photographs of steam trains exist looking down on this bridge as the locomotives made tremendous efforts to cross from the watershed between the Afon Iaen (Dyfi Valley) and the Afon Carno (Severn Valley). Arriva Cyrmu lost the tender for this route to Lloyds Coaches in August 2005. *Author (2005)*

The villagers have a tradition of open shelters. Arriva Midlands North service 71 stops in the centre of Arddleen/Arddlîn (flax garden or rettery) at 2.40 pm on the route from Oswestry via Guilsfield to Welshpool. The Montgomeryshire canal is immediately behind the houses close to the branch canal to Guilsfield. The Gilbert Scott-designed telephone kiosk still stands. Most kiosks in the county are modern or have closed. *Author (2005)*

The Dennis Dart waits in a section set aside for coaches to park prior to drawing into the bay at the bus station at Newtown. This will be the Arriva Cymru service to Machynlleth departing at 4.00 pm. Kuldev Singh stands by the public information message on the rear of the bus that encourages people to ask in Welsh first if they can. Kuldev can reply in Welsh, English or Punjabi. He also has his turban in the same colour as the bus body. Kuldev was working his notice for another job. The bus route would transfer to Lloyds Coaches within six weeks. *Author (2005)*

The Arriva Cymru Dennis waits at Machynlleth to depart to Dolgellau on the coast route via Aberdyfi, Twwyn and Fairbourne. The bus has details of the Bangor to Aberystwyth TrawsCambria route on the side plus details of the £5 per day rover on the lower panels. There are two bus stops set either side in the wide section of the street close to the town centre.
Author (2004)

A Sunday photograph shows Arriva Midlands North buses parked at the Abermule yard. This was part of the railway sidings of the Abermule station and the buses leave the yard on what was the track of the Kerry branch line railway. *Author (2005)*

This factory was owned by Phillips Cycles after the war, then BRD making car and lorry transmissions and was to become the Lions Works in the early 1980s. G. Owens & Sons rapidly diversified from coal from the railway wharf to become a major haulier with heavy vehicle workshops for themselves and other local companies. The 21-year-old Leyland 6-80 is still in Beadles colours but is now owned by Les Skilton, mechanic driver for Beadles and now succesor. The senior fitter, Roy Poston, trained by Mid-Wales Motorways in the late 1950s will soon place the reconditioned engine into the mid-mounted underfloor position. The bus is on concrete built on the stone base from the Glog Quarry. *Author (2006)*

The Arriva Scania with Plaxton Paladin body stops at Abermule on the last day of operation by the company, 28th October, 2006. The bus stop is about 100 yards from the long-closed Abermule station. *Author (2006)*

Postscript

Several changes always occur between research and the final preparation for publication. A number of historical photographs can always be added. Much of the recent information would be the normal succession and transfer within companies and slight changes to services. There have been several significant changes and these follow with illustrations.

The reduction in postbus routes. A massacre or an elegy could be a better description of what has happened. The initial services in 1967 such as Llanidloes to Llangurig were based on grants, fuel subsidy, etc. Rural post services have been subjected to rapid change including the use of e-mail with reduction of postal deliveries and collections. The older local people with no driving licence have passed on. Many incomers now seek a rural home as long distance commuters based on multiple car ownership causing house prices to become too expensive for local rural workers. The county councils are cash strapped, the number using the postbuses have fallen so it has become increasingly difficult to justify services. The Llanidloes to Llangurig and Dylife services quietly died in August 2006 and most of these rural services in Wales have now ceased.

The return of the brand name of TrawsCambria. The origin was with Crosville Motors where the Cardiff to Wrexham/Chester coach was timed to meet with the Bangor to Cheltenham coach at Newtown bus station with toilets and a cafe. The new service is Newtown to Brecon via Llandrindod replacing the long lost Moat Lane to Brecon rail service. There are six daily services, Monday to Saturday. The service is operated by Stagecoach in South Wales with the head office at Cwmbran near Newport. The other services with the brand name are Bangor to Aberystwyth, Barmouth to Wrexham, Aberystwyth to Carmarthen and Cardigan with connections to Cardiff, Abergavenny to Cardiff via Brecon & Merthyr and Llandovery to Brecon. All use easy access buses.

Future legislation requires the provision of low-floor buses with access for people in wheel chairs. Bus manufacturers, bus companies and county support services are therefore phasing these in. These include services operating in Powys. The contracts have caused changes. They include Lloyds who operate the Newtown to Machynlleth service and Tanat Valley Coaches who have the contract for Llanidloes to Shrewsbury Services. These were operated by Crosville in the 1980s and inherited by Arriva Cymru and Arriva Midlands North. All these services use Optare new buses. Owens of Oswestry offer such services in Newtown and Welshpool while Crossgate Motors offer the same facility from Llandrindod. Many of these services are timed to connect with the Traws Cambria and with railway stations.

European legislation determines tendering that is transparent and open to all within the European Community. This has an effect of postal services making it more difficult to cross-subsidise post buses. A new name has appeared competing for school contracts. Veolia Cymru Ltd has some successful tenders starting in June 2007. The company already operates a number of stage services within the South Wales conurbations. It contains several successful coach companies including Shamrock and the long-established Bebbs. It therefore contains staff with experience of local bus operation. The company has French capital and traded previously with the Connex brand. The initial Powys contracts are

Four Optare Tempos in a row show the plan to inter-change routes. The nearest is Lloyds with the Newtown to Machynlleth route, the next is the TrawsCambria with the Newtown to Brecon service then the final two are Tanat Valley Coaches with the Llanidloes to Shrewsbury and the Shrewsbury to Llanidloes services all timed to connect at Newtown bus station. There are connections at Llandrindod for Hereford, Machynlleth for Bangor, Aberystwyth and Carmarthen. The bus park will also have the Dennis Plaxton town service and the Kerry minibus. The rail connections can also take place. *Author (2006)*

First day of operation by Tanat Valley Coaches, 30th October, 2006, shows one of the brand new Optare Tempos at Newtown bus station. The cantals are English on one side and Welsh on the opposite side so Amwythig is Shrewsbury, Y Trallwng is Welshpool, Y Drenewydd is Newtown and Llanidloes is both. *Author (2006)*

The postbus waits in the Newtown Post Office yard at 3.45 pm prior to departure to New Mills at 4.00 pm. One lady already rests on the rear seat. Seating had been reduced to eight so any postman could drive the unit. In 2007, only 10 to 15 customers used the service per week, virtually all have free bus passes. This was one of the few postbus services to continue in Powys in 2007, all services were withdrawn in April 2009. *Author (2007)*

mainly within Ystradgynlais in South West Brecon. The company has given a commitment to local depots, to local staff and to the Welsh language. The immediate question is why Veolia (also Crosville and Arriva) when there is no V in the Welsh language? The local small companies have protested virulently including demonstrations at County Hall. The situation remains undetermined in the first month of this new name operating in Powys. The problem of capital provision for a school bus remains unsolved for successful tenders have always been based on skilled use of older buses. The political concept of parental choice of school has led to much increase in bus, taxi and private transport. This has led to a percentage increase in school transport provision that is expensive in a remote rural area. It remains to be seen if our future mobility can be maintained with oil difficulties, climate change and other factors.

The historic Mid-Wales Motorways bus depot has been demolished as the site became part of a Tesco supermarket development. A full inspection of the Roman road between Caersws and Forden/Wroxeter was carried out by archaeologists. The Mid Wales Travel services at Newtown transferred to Tanat Valley Motors. Tanat Valley had already taken on the old site of Corfields Lorry Transport at Kerry for service and valeting. The number of buses now exceeded the planning permission for the site so Tanat Valley have once more stabled some vehicles at the old Abermule sidings. All this took place in early summer of 2009. Tanat Valley now has two substantial depots at Llanrhaeadr for North East Montgomeryshire and at Kerry for the Upper Severn valley services.

Mid-Wales Motorways had formed in 1937 and used this site from 1947 until 2009. Les Skilton, who transferred to Tanat Valley Coaches, closes the entrance gate for the final time. *David Hughes, Pontrobert/Shrewsbury*

Knills of Crossgate Motors near Llandrindod (ex-Crosville to 1954) sold its company to Veolia Transport Cymru. Many of the Radnorshire services are now in Veolia livery. Veolia livery can be seen in Montgomeryshire at Llanidloes on route 47 (Builth, Llandrindod, Rhayader, Llanidloes service with connections timed for Newtown, Brecon and Aberystwyth) and a new service on route 41 at Newtown connecting Kington, Presteigne, Knighton and Newtown.

Veolia have some Powys contracts within Montgomeryshire but these isolates are contracted to Tanat Valley. It includes the reintroduction of the 1930s Cookson's service between Newtown and Welshpool via Montgomery.

Sadly, the final Royal Mail postbus in Powys and Wales ceased in April 2009. The route from Newtown to New Mills just faded away.

There has been some increased services with Lloyds Coaches based at Machynlleth for both Gwynedd and Powys. This include several extras to Newtown.

Owens of Oswestry has improved both the Newtown and Welshpool town service frequencies using BMC (Turkey) short-wheelbased buses. Its head office is in Oswestry but its bus depot is at Four Crosses in Montgomeryshire. One of its inherited drivers, David Percival , has retired after 40 plus years bus work. David has worked for Beadles, Mid Wales Travel, Crosville and Stratos, often on the Newtown services. He has given quiet advice throughout this project and this has been valued.

A Conclusion

The story commenced with a request from the local historical society to interview an older long-standing friend on the day Mid-Wales Motorways was created in 1937. This was done in late 2003. Oakwood Press suggested that there could be a bus volume. This gave the impetus to gather the necessary material from around April 2004 to December 2005. The collection is a local story for people who have lived in Montgomeryshire, and for many who come to the area and enjoy exploring a very rich history of human endeavour. It is a bonus if others interested in the bus/coach industry find the story of the network of independents in one of the least populated areas of Britain of interest.

A report in 2005 by the Welsh Consumer Council suggests that one in three people in Wales are on the wrong side of the transport divide. They are denied what many others take for granted such as a late return from seeing a film or easy access to friends. Over the last 50 years, the use of the car has transformed society allowing a wider choice of work and travel whenever needed. Railway line closure and bus service decline have resulted in certain groups with real problems of getting to health centres, hospitals etc. The rural areas have a larger percentage of car ownership but the average age of cars is around nine years suggesting that those struggling within lower social economic groups keep mobility by 'marginal' motoring to get to work.

Therefore a continual theme throughout this research is that of financial viability. Many worked within the parish community in the late 1940s. A bus to the nearest town on both market day and Saturday plus some private hire such as Sunday school trips and excursions to a larger town or seaside met the needs of a society where most could not afford a car. The same parish in 2005 will have lost many farming, forestry and quarry jobs with mechanization. The opportunity for women has widened beyond any concept of a rural society that offered working in service, the cook/caretaker for the local school, farm work or housewife. The car has suburbanized even the remote uplands with second homes, retirement, caravan parks and commuting. Many now work with a service industry from a computer base and visit their company office as required. Each decade sees a debate on the accepted 'universality' of maintaining rural access. Some have asked what will be the future as information of services past is recorded. The use of stage routes has grown recently within the area but this growth is heavily dependent on the free pass for pensioners and other concessions. It can therefore alter with a change in what support is possible from the tax/ratepayer. Rural transport is not isolated from congestion etc. The main road between Caersws and Welshpool is congested in the peak morning and afternoon rush. Parking is a problem both for work and for the village and small town spaces at weekends and evenings. Congestion can be chronic on Fridays as those with second homes, those who return from work for the weekend to their families and the caravans to the coast all pile through roads that have adequate space for maybe 95 per cent of the week.

It is therefore likely that local coach and bus services plus the few railway lines will be maintained. The question of future fuel supply, global warming etc. may also produce a technological and social change that cannot be predicted. The extreme mobility of the last few decades has been dependent upon cheap fuel and cheap mass-produced cars so it may be necessary to have another model in the future. Whatever happens, it is likely that an independent proprietor will carve out a niche for his or her coach company to continue. Someone should be able to construct an update of the history of the buses of Montgomeryshire 2005 to 2050 and the material should contain a range of unusual services and buses. The use of double-decks has never been common in the area in the past. It is unlikely that a cascaded down 'bendy' bus will therefore be common in rural Britain in the future.

The final paragraph is to record a huge thanks to everyone who has made a contribution. It has been a delight to spend time with some of the older people as they recall grandfather (*taid*) and his bus company from their childhood memory of the 1930s. The current proprietors and their staff have made much effort to collect their record and photographs. They have also encouraged the effort to keep going when my enthusiasm flagged. Many others have helped with reading, corrections, suggested dates for change and all the other myriad activities that become part of such a project. The county is 'thin' for collecting passengers. Low population density gives few bookshops so it is hoped that enough locals will be willing to buy a book on 'buses'. Whatever happens, it has been a most enjoyable experience collecting the necessary information. There have been a number of Montgomeryshire books that contain much information on the drovers, the turnpikes, the canal and the railways. Welcome to the first one on buses/coaches.

One of the Tanat Valley coaches is used to show low floor easy access to enhance mobility. Muriel Penlington of Newtown demonstrates use. *Author (2006)*

Bibliography

Much of the material within this volume has been recorded for the first time. The technique has been time consuming spending time visiting the older people connected with the Montgomeryshire bus/coach industry. The author is approaching 70 years of age and material recorded in 2005 must reflect all that has passed such as travel during childhood wartime austerity but it has been seen as it was in 2005. Articles of 1950 assume that the industry will remain prosperous, articles of the 1960s worry about future rural transport and articles of the 1970s assume that the National Bus Company is part of the solution. The following have been useful during the research.

Llawllyfr Teithio Powys/Powys Travel Guide contains public transport timetables and route maps for the County. It is updated annually. Both Gwynedd and Shropshire Guides were valued.

A History of Crosville Motor Services by A.C. Anderson (David & Charles)

Crosville Motor Services 1, The First 40 years by J. Carroll and D. Roberts (Venture Publications)

Crosville Motor Services 2, 1945 to 1990 by D. Roberts (NBC Books)

Crosville, The Successors 1986 to 2001 by D. Roberts (NBC Books)

Bedford Volume 1, 1923 to 1950 by S. Broach & A. Townsin (Venture Publications)

The Bedford Story 2, 1950 to 1986 by S. Broach & A. Townsin (Venture Publications)

Halcyon Days of Buses Charles Klapper Collection/Omnibus Society (Ian Allan)

British Buses before 1945 by J. Aldridge (Ian Allan)

The British Motor Bus, by G. Booth (Ian Allan)

The History of British Bus Services by J. Hibbs (David & Charles)

The Country Bus by J. Hibbs (David & Charles)

Welsh Bus Handbook/National Express Handbook/Arriva Bus Handbook (British Bus Publishing)

Random testing (brakes, lights, exhaust etc.) is part of the remit in addition to the comprehensive station test. The best site for a random test is to check vehicles as they arrive for school contracts. This is at Llanfair Caereinion. Vehicle maintenance is of a high standard considering the problem of many older vehicles. The nearest coach is from Geraint Gittins (Dolanog), the vehicle partially hidden behind is from Selwyn Hughes (Llanfair) and the bus on the curve is from Gwyn Jones (Meifod). *Malcolm Yeoman, Pontrobert/Llandrindod*

Index